The Evidence For God

T0155395

The Evidence For God

The Case for the Existence of the Spiritual
Dimension

Keith Ward

DARTON · LONGMAN + TODD

First published in 2014 by
Darton, Longman and Todd Ltd
1 Spencer Court
140 – 142 Wandsworth High Street
London SW18 4JJ

ISBN 978-0-232-53130-5

A catalogue record for this book is available from the British Library

Phototypeset by Kerrypress Ltd, Luton, Beds
Printed and bound in Great Britain by Bell & Bain, Glasgow

CONTENTS

1.

THE SPIRITUAL
DIMENSION

Does a spiritual dimension exist?

It is remarkable how atheism is becoming fashionable in England. It has become almost compulsory to say that you do not believe in God, if you are to stay abreast of fashion. It is equally remarkable that very few people have any idea of what great spiritual teachers have said about God. Knowledge of God is confined to a few stereotypical ideas about an invisible person living just outside the universe who interferes in it from time to time, and who long ago dictated a few ethical commands to groups of nomadic peasants, commands which can now be seen to be thoroughly irrational and obsolete.

What many people in our culture seem to have lost is any sense that there is more to reality than collections of physical particles accidentally arranged in complicated patterns. I have spent a lot of my time in recent years talking to sixth formers (eighteen-year-olds in British schools) about philosophy and religion. I have found that for more than half of them, even at schools with a religious foundation, any sort of religion or spiritual practice is a closed book. They think that the whole universe is some sort of gigantic accident, that there are no objective moral values, and that belief in anything like God is a bit of comforting self-deception.

Atheism and what you might call 'accidentalism' (that everything is an accident, or is due to pure chance) is usually just a default position. It is what is taken for granted without argument, though there is often some vague feeling that this is what 'scientists' have proved.

When I talk to eminent scientists some of them do support this sort of position. Time and again they have said to me, 'There is no evidence for God'. They think that God is an unnecessary addition to reality, which does not have any useful function, and can be dropped without losing anything much. They often quote Bertrand Russell's remark that believing in God is like believing that there is an invisible and intangible teapot in orbit around the earth. Nobody can see it or touch it, and it does not make any difference to anything, but some people just seem to believe it is there 'on faith', or without any evidence. God, they think, is like that.

I should stress that it is only some scientists who say this sort of thing, but they tend to be the most publicly visible scientists (like David Attenborough and Professor Brian Cox – not that they have ever discussed invisible teapots). They appear on TV and are reported widely in the press, and what they say is taken as true by many young people. The two I have mentioned have done a tremendous amount to introduce people to the wonders of nature, and I could not admire them more. Yet I think they are quite wrong when they discount spirituality. I also believe that science itself points in a very different direction. There is a huge amount of evidence for the reality of a spiritual dimension to the world, and human life is going to be very different if the idea of God (or some idea very like it, an idea of a spiritual dimension to human life) disappears. But the fact that there is a huge amount of evidence has become so little recognised that it is going to have to be argued for.

What is spirit?

First of all we need to get some idea of what I mean by 'a spiritual dimension', and what the great majority of philosophers in world history, both East and West, have said about it, so that we know what we are talking about. It is a rather vague phrase. It is purposely so, because I do not want to get bogged down in all sorts of arguments about the exact nature of God, or about some dogmatic belief that all people are supposed to accept. What I am talking about is the sense that the universe we live in and know a little about is more than just a collection of material particles or fields or waves (whatever exactly you prefer) with no consciousness, no objective value, no purpose, and no meaning. There is also a level of being that is deeper, that has something like purpose and value, and we humans can sometimes feel it and find in it resources of strength, hope, and inspiration. There is something like mind or consciousnessness at the heart of reality. I do not want to tie this down too much in words. As the Chinese spiritual classic the *Tao Te Ching* says, 'The Tao that can be spoken is not the eternal Tao'.

We need not know too much about the inner nature of matter (and perhaps nobody does, really) in order to find our way around the material world, and use it to fulfil our material needs. In the same way, we do not need to know too much about the inner nature of spirit (something non-material, but conscious, mind-like in some way, and of greater than purely human value) in order to realise that we live in a spiritual environment as well as a material one, and that to become attuned to that environment is to unlock huge resources of power and love in our lives. In fact, despite what I have said about the 'default position' of atheism in English, and maybe in European culture, there is also, I believe, a huge interest in spirituality, and a very widespread sense that there is an important spiritual dimension to human life. The trouble is that there is very rarely any way of holding together the fashionable intellectual atheism of the day and the deep sense of a spiritual dimension of human life.

Most philosophers and thinkers, especially in the Western traditions, have spoken about this spiritual depth as 'God'. Others, however, especially perhaps Buddhists, regard that term as too anthropomorphic and limited (it is a personal and masculine term, after all). They use other terms, like 'Pure Mind', or 'Suchness' or even 'the Ultimate'. I will continue to use the word God – it is a nice short word – but I want to say very clearly that I am really talking about spiritual values, and about the sense of spirituality, which I take to be a concern with values of the mind and heart, values which really exist in reality, and which are felt to be higher than the values of any purely human mind. So I will also speak of 'Spirit', thinking of these values as known by some sort of non-human consciousness, and thus as existing in something more like a mind than like a stone or a tree – though something very unlike any human mind.

Almost all great philosophers, theologians, and spiritual writers, agree that God is just one way, and a particularly personal way, of speaking of Spirit. God is *not* a male person with a beard, sitting on a throne somewhere above the sky, or perhaps just outside the universe. Still, God is personal, and I am not going to assume that there is a personal God, or that all people with a spiritual sense believe they are encountering such a personal God. Nevertheless, many of them do. In fact many religious writers – sometimes called 'mystics' (though that word can be very misleading) – hardly think of God as personal or male or like human minds at all. One of the most famous definitions of God – among philosophers, anyway – was given by Anselm, who was the Archbishop of Canterbury in the eleventh century. He said God is 'that than which nothing greater can be conceived'.[1]

On this definition, God is a unique sort of reality which is more worth-while, of greater value, more worth knowing and contemplating just for its own sake, than anything else anyone can think of. Just what that reality would be is something we have to work out for ourselves by asking what we think the most worth-while or valuable thing we imagine would be like. We might not be able to think of anything – in which case we will have no idea of God. If so, maybe we should just try harder. Different people might have different ideas of the most worth-while possible thing. Some will think of a personal being, even of a person. Others will think of an impersonal being, like Plato's 'the Good', perhaps. Some will think of a being that constantly creates and changes. Others will think of a completely changeless and timeless being. There is plenty of room for disagreement. But most people will at least think of a reality which is more beautiful, more wise, more powerful, and more compassionate, than we are.

Of course, while this is a very famous definition, it does not follow that there really is a 'greatest conceivable thing', even though Anselm had a very irritating argument – the so-called 'Ontological argument' - to prove that there was, an argument which nobody believes but nobody can finally refute either. You can, after all, believe in a spiritual reality which is very great, but not able to do absolutely anything, and so not quite the 'greatest conceivable being'. I want to think about such slightly lower-level spiritual realities too, and that is one reason why I will not always use the word 'God'. But I will start with Anselm's definition as the boldest and most interesting one, and later see whether it may need modifying when we compare it with the actual universe that we observe. Maybe it is worth pointing out, from the start, that Anselm's God is probably not very like either a kindly and indulgent father or like a domineering tyrant either. We might spell out the idea of a 'greatest conceivable being' in a number of different ways, and they will probably not include either of these extreme and rather naive ideas. It is partly for that reason that I will sometimes use the rather less emotionally loaded word 'Spirit' instead.

It does not seem very likely that Spirit will be a person. Of course, if you think the most perfect possible thing is a person, it will seem likely to you. But even then it will be very different from a human person. Human persons have very limited power and knowledge, and are always making mistakes and doing things that are not very good. A personal spirit will have power unlimited by any other being and knowledge greater than that of any other being, will never make mistakes, and whatever it intends to do will be good (because the most worth-while possible being will always do very worth-while things). As Anselm said, God will actually be not just the greatest thing we can think of, but is likely to be much greater, much more perfect, than anything we can think of. So some people might say that Spirit is personal, but is much greater than any person, as we understand human persons.

Will Spirit have a body? That is, will it be a material thing, located somewhere in space, perhaps beyond the stars? Anselm thought not, and modern science would agree. There is a law in modern science, the second law of thermodynamics, which says that everything in the universe runs down eventually. Every material thing in our universe sooner or later decays, and in billions of years the whole universe will cease to exist. If you think about it, it is obviously better not to decay and cease to exist. So if Spirit is the greatest conceivable being, or even, perhaps, the greatest thing there actually is, it will not be part of the material universe. Spirit will not be part of our space and time. Spirit will be non-material or spiritual. If it exists at all, it will be more like consciousness or mind. That is one way of describing God, but just to avoid arguments, I will not insist that everyone should call it God.

Believing in Spirit, then, is not believing that there is some sort of invisible person who interferes in arbitrary ways with the universe, for instance finding car-parking-spaces for his favourite people who ask very nicely, or sending earthquakes on people he especially dislikes. Believing in Spirit is believing that there is an existing state or reality of vast knowledge, understanding, freedom, beauty and happiness, not located anywhere in physical space, a spiritual reality of supreme value. Spirit will be supremely desirable and supremely worthy of reverence and admiration. This is not because it wants or needs our worship, as if worship was some sort of abject fawning. It is just because the natural response to such a being is one of awe, wonder, and admiration. If there is a Spirit, and if we could really become acquainted with it in some way, we could not help worshipping it, as the most beautiful and awe-inspiring being we could imagine.

It should be clear that looking for evidence for God, or for Spirit, or for spiritual reality, is not going to be like looking for evidence for some exotic animal or for an invisible teapot. Looking for that sort of evidence is like looking for footprints, or chewed leaves that will show an animal has been there. But a purely spiritual being does not leave footprints or chew leaves. If you wonder whether there is a reality of supreme understanding, beauty, and bliss, you are not going to find that out by looking for visible marks that some physical object makes. Spirit is not a physical object, so we will not be looking for evidence for something physical.

There can be evidence for spiritual things, but it will not be like evidence for physical objects. Even when physicists look for evidence for tiny sub-atomic particles that can never be observed, like quarks, they assume those particles are physical in some sense. They have location in space, they move about in space, and they have physical impacts on other particles. Spirit is not like that. The main and most important evidence for Spirit will be evidence for the existence of non-physical supreme values. There is such evidence, but it is going to be very unlike evidence for electrons or quarks. Maybe that is why some scientists say there is no evidence for God or for spiritual reality. They are imagining, wrongly, that there is some sort of physical thing (made of very thin or transparent matter, perhaps), which might leave tracks in a cloud –chamber, or tell-tale marks on a computer screen. But Spirit is not physical at all. So it is not surprising that there is no evidence *of that sort*. A different sort of evidence is needed.

Looking for evidence for spiritual values

What sort of evidence could there be for a spiritual, non-physical, reality of supreme value? When we ask for evidence, we are usually thinking of some physical marks or traces. Are there any physical marks or traces of a supremely valuable being in the universe as we experience it? I am sure that there are, but there is a problem. Not everyone would agree about such evidence. Some people see the universe as cruel and violent; some see it as just boring and uninteresting; some see it as just 'one damn thing after another'.

Some people even commit suicide, because they cannot face existing in a universe like this.

We have to respect such feelings. They are personal and deeply emotional responses to the world as we experience it. We do not, after all, see our experience as experience of a neutral world. We see it as charged with feeling-elements, with dangers, threats, beauties and terrors. 'All knowledge begins with experience', said British Empiricist philosophers like Hume and Locke and Berkeley.[2] I agree with that, and if we are going to find any evidence for spiritual reality, we will have to begin with experience. But it is not at all obvious what 'experience' is. It usually comes through our senses – sight, touch, sound, taste, and smell. But is it confined to things like colours, shapes, noises, and touches? Obviously not, because we say that our senses 'tell us' that there is a world of three-dimensional solid objects out there. Our sense-impressions communicate information about a physical external world.

But is that all they do? Some philosophers, like the well-known English philosopher A. J. Ayer (who once tried to teach me) have tried to separate feelings completely from sense-perceptions. He suggested that our sense-perceptions (which he called 'sense-data') tell us about a world of facts, which are neither good nor bad, neither beautiful nor ugly. They just are. Then we react to things, by purely subjective responses of liking or disliking. These are subjective feelings, Ayer said, because they do not really belong to the things themselves. They are just reactions we happen to have to things. They are not objective properties of the things themselves. Different people have different feeling reactions to things. Such reactions are purely subjective, and tell us nothing about the real world.[3]

But is that true? Do our feelings tell us nothing about the world? After all, if we see a lion approaching us rather rapidly, we do not say that we first have some perfectly objective lion-shaped visual perceptions, and then we have a purely subjective feeling of fear. Lions really are threatening, and we do not just see some perfectly neutral sense-data. We perceive a real threat, and the feeling of fear is part of that perception. Feelings are part of our experience. So if we find the world depressing or pointless, or if we find it beautiful and exciting, this is not just our subjective reaction to our experience. It is part of how we experience the world, part of how it appears to us.

Of course, people experience the world in different ways. But then they perceive the world in different ways too. You just cannot separate off your perceptions completely from your feeling-responses to the world, and say that one is objective and the other is not. What is really out there is, of course, seen from your own point of view. But that does not mean it is not real. It is what is real, from your point of view.

When you think about it, your perceptions are not really of 'things', independently existing solid objects, after all (well, not according to the Empiricists' official doctrine, anyway). All our perceptions – the sights, sounds, smells, touches, and tastes that we have – are in a way 'subjective' too. They are not really properties of separately existing things, and we can never even be really sure that 'things' exist, when we are not looking at them.

We know that the sights, sounds, and so on that we have are constructed by the mind, and are not 'pictures' of real things out there. Electro-magnetic vibrations of waves with a frequency between the infra-red and the ultra-violet hit the retinas of our eyes, cause electro-chemical impulses to race to about thirty different areas of our brains, which then produce a picture of three dimensional solid coloured objects. But anybody who knows about the physiology of perception knows that this picture is a construct which the mind fills in from data which are very different in reality.

So what makes us think that our so-called 'subjective reactions' are not just as real and 'objective' as our sense-perceptions are? Might our feelings not tell us, just as our sense-perceptions do, something about the world we experience? Feelings are constructed by the mind, just as our perceptions are, so who is to say that they do not reflect something about the reality we encounter in experience?

Our point of view might not be a very good one. It may be clouded by all sorts of preconceptions and inaccurate beliefs. But it is still a point of view of something out there. It is not just a fantasy conjured up by our minds which has no relation to what is real. Of course there are fantasies and delusions. But the very fact that we call them fantasies shows that we are able to distinguish normal beliefs and fantasies. Not all our beliefs about the world can be fantasies. The hard problem is to find a reliable way of making the distinction between reality and delusion. But that there is a distinction to be made is not in doubt.

If you accept this you might say that our feelings normally, when they are working properly, give us a special sort of access to reality. They reveal values (things that we admire and love) and disvalues (things that we fear and dislike) to us. Human knowledge is not a sort of mechanical registering of information, with values being added on as an after-thought to what we perceive. Human knowledge is essentially experience of values and disvalues, so that we perceive things related to us in threatening or inspiring ways, to which we may be more or less sensitive, depending on our own preconceptions and ways of relating to the world. This is where we might start looking for evidence of spiritual values.

It seems reasonable to say that all human knowledge begins with experience, and that our experience is of values that we seem to perceive as somehow there in reality. Human knowledge is not just the recording of neutral facts or sense-perceptions. If we explore various areas of human experience where we seem to encounter such objective values, we might find that these are values that really exist whether we acknowledge them or not. We perceive them from our own personal point of view, with all our inherited and learned prejudices, special interests, and capabilities. But they can reveal to us something important about reality.

In the following sections of this book, I will look at six main areas of human experience: at the arts, at morality, at philosophy, at science, at religion, and at personal experience. In each area, I will try to show that there are special experiences of values, and that these experiences are evidence for the existence of more than simply physical facts, even though they are closely related to physical facts. When you take all these areas together, the evidence builds up to an impressive argument for seeing the world that we experience as communicating spiritual values – a 'sense for the spiritual dimension', that is beyond and yet expressed in and through physical facts.

Not everybody would associate this spiritual sense with God. That is partly because many people think of God as a rather nasty or despotic person who stops people doing what they want, and is often angry and vindictive. We might set aside such an idea of God, however, and think of God, as Anselm did, as the most perfect and desirable being there could possibly be. Then we could say that believing in God is believing that all the different objective spiritual values we experience are expressions of one reality of supreme value, which is the source of all the values we can experience. This is what the philosopher Plato called 'the Good-and-Beautiful'. Plato thought that *philokalia*, the love of the good and beautiful, is the highest human activity.[4] 'The Good' is also, with some slight amendments, what most theologians and philosophers have called God. It is what I am calling Spirit.

I want to argue that if we put it like that, there are lots of human experiences that are, taken together, good evidence for Spirit. But of course to accept that means that we have to interpret our experiences in a special way, as experiences of a transcendent spiritual dimension. Not everybody will do that. We would have to cultivate a special sensibility, the spiritual sense, to do it. So the evidence is not convincing evidence for everybody. All the same, it is evidence. And it is enough to make belief in Spirit a reasonable and fulfilling part of our mental life. Belief in Spirit will not be a mere leap of faith without any supporting evidence. It will be a fully rational and sensitive approach to the richest and most important parts of human experience.

2.

SPIRITUAL VALUES IN ART AND BEAUTY

Art as 'mediating evidence'

I will begin by looking at the sense of beauty, which we find both in nature and in art. Painting, sculpture, music, drama, literature, and dance are all forms of art, of creating beautiful forms that can be contemplated and enjoyed just for their own sake. Art can have a sense of meaning and value that seems to convey a sense of transcendence, of something conveyed in and through physical forms, yet having a reality that is more than just physical. This sense can be experienced in two main ways, in the creative process of composing artistic works, and in the contemplative process of enjoying and appreciating them. Artistic creativity and appreciation are two of the main values that reveal a spiritual dimension of life to humans, two major forms of spiritual value.

The ancient Greeks spoke of the Muses as inspiring goddesses who helped them to create beautiful forms. Many artists through the ages have felt a power of inspiration that seems to work through them, almost to use them to bring into being new forms of beauty. When an artist creates a new work of art, he or she naturally works within a tradition which has been built up over many years. Yet traditions constantly change and develop, sometimes in novel ways, and originality of vision and technique is a quality greatly prized in artists. Great art is the bringing into being of the new, of something never seen before, constructed by the sheer power of creativity.

Such creativity is a human capacity, possessed in many different degrees by different people. Yet in a way it can seem more than human, as if the skill and training of a particular artist becomes a channel for a new vision of beauty to take shape in the world, for a new form of beauty to become actual. Not all art is beautiful or novel or even competent. It takes a special skill and genius to produce great art. But when that happens – in a Mozart symphony or a Raphael painting – human creativity becomes the vehicle of something amazingly valuable, something worthy of reverence and awe, delight and admiration, just for its own sake. Such creativity is a gift, and it is given to few – though most of us can imitate it at a much less creative and original level. Great art is a revelation, an unveiling of possibilities of beauty that we had not seen, that even the artist had not seen until it flowed out in times - sometimes rare and elusive, sometimes pouring out almost endlessly - of inspired creativity.

There can be here a sense of 'possession' by a more than human power of creativity, using human talents and possibilities to unveil depths of meaning and value in reality that seem completely new. I am not claiming that this process of creative possession is religious. I am pointing out that, for many, it is something that gives new meaning and value to existence, that 'uses' human talents, and that can give real and vitalising purpose to human life. Even for those who are not primarily creative artists, works of art can reveal values which give to human experience an intrinsic worth and fulfilment.

When we look at a painting, we may just see it as a set of two-dimensional coloured patches, which is what it is. But is that ALL that it is? Absolutely not! The patches represent something, perhaps a figure or a landscape. But is that all they do? If so, a photograph would do the job better. What a good painting conveys is what the painter has seen in the subject that is painted, and the meaning the painter wants, perhaps not fully consciously, to convey. Paintings express feelings, but not in any obvious way. It takes a practised art-critic to try to bring out what great paintings convey. And if you have read more than one art-critic, you will know that each critic 'sees' different meanings in a painting. There is not just one meaning, which you either get right or wrong. Bringing your own perspective to a painting will reveal new meanings in it. Are those meanings really there? That is an odd question. 'What is really there' is a very complex combination of what is in the subject of the painting, what the painter saw and was able to convey, what various critics have seen, and what the observer sees, or fails to see, in the visual display that is objectively there.

The average viewing time of the *Mona Lisa* in the Louvre in Paris, is three seconds, because you are pressed onwards by the crowd behind you. What do we get from that? It might be, 'I have seen a great and iconic painting. I can tick it off my list'. It might be, 'The technique is magnificent, and I can learn from it how to paint'. Or 'A very nice portrait of a young woman's smile'. Or ' A work which somehow conveys the subtlety, complexity, and veiled enigma of a human personality'. Is one of those the right response? Some are more perceptive than others, we might say. But it does not seem right to say that there is one 'correct' response.

Paintings, of course, are not like lions. You may perceive lions as fearsome, and that is a feeling-apprehension which partly depends upon your own feelings about lions. But whatever your feelings are, lions will eat you. They really are to be feared, and such a feeling is highly appropriate. Paintings will not eat you. If you see a painting as hideous and ugly, there is nothing it will do to you. That is why many people say that our feelings about art are purely subjective, not about real features of the world at all.

It is, however, possible to learn more about art, even art you dislike. There are more and less appropriate reactions to art. You will never eliminate disagreements. Personal tastes and interests will always differ to some extent. Indeed, that is part of learning about art, to discover how other people see things, and how their insights can complement our own. We learn also, however, that there are some gulfs of understanding that are so deep that we do not know how to cross them.

That does not mean it is all wholly subjective. It means that what you see in works of art depends partly on your own personality, and also upon your cultural training and previous experiences. It is the same in all sense-perception, though to a lesser degree than in art. You do not register some sense-perceptions, and afterwards react subjectively to them. Your sense-perceptions are, from the start, apprehended with pleasure or aversion, with fascination or boredom.

But is that all there is to it? Pleasure or aversion? I would think that such a view demeans and misunderstands great art, as it demeans great music and great literature. There are depths to be experienced, but experience of them demands a certain personal discernment and sensitivity. Even though there is no one 'right' view, some views are shallow, and others reveal depths that cannot easily, or at all, be put into words, but they can change your whole understanding of human existence.

You have to learn to appreciate art, to see what there is in it. You have to cultivate your sensitivity to what is there to be seen. And when you do that, you are not just seeing the purely empirical or physical features that are undoubtedly present. You are discerning meaning and value, expressed in and through those physical features.

It is a bit like reading a text. When you read a book, you do not just notice the physical shape and spacing of the letters. In fact you are probably not aware of them at all. You read words, units of meaning, and you understand something *by means of* the physical marks on a page. The physical marks are mediators of meaning. That is their function, without which they have no point.

Understanding meaning is a partly a function of your personal discrimination, sensitivity, and judgment. Such things can be taught, but in the end some people are just more perceptive and sensitive to particular works than others. We say of them, 'They can see things in this that I could never have seen. They can help me to see those things in a new way'. Art deepens and enriches human experience. The appreciation of art gives many human lives a significance and importance that would otherwise be lacking.

The spiritual dimension in art

I want to suggest that in the creation and appreciation of art there is a sort of 'spiritual perception', a sensitivity to non-material factors that are communicated through physical perceptions. For some people, such appreciation is the most important thing in their lives. We may say, 'Art is their religion'. But it is, taken on its own, a rather odd sort of religion. It often lacks any very obvious moral or intellectual dimension. It concentrates on feeling rather than on morally responsible action or a great interest in consistency and coherence of thought. We do not expect great artists to be saints or sages. But they have insights into human existence which reveal things many of us would not otherwise have known.

Great art teaches us that there is something in reality to be known by those who learn to see it, or who have the natural ability to see it. It is more than pure physical data. In art we can create and discern objective and intrinsic values. Such values are objective, because they are more than merely subjective responses to data which are in themselves value-neutral. Such values are intrinsic, in that they are worth-while just for their own sake. They are not values because we happen to like them. They are values which it is good to discern and appreciate. In ordinary human experience, and in the enhanced experience that art provides, you know something that is more than either value-free sense-perceptions or merely physical elements. Yet it is essentially expressed in and through the physical and sense-observed. That 'in and through', the sense of something transcendent, 'beyond', yet expressed in the particular, is the sense of objective value. It is a sense for the spiritual dimension.

Is art evidence of objective value? The word 'evidence' sounds odd, because evidence usually consists of physical traces from which you can infer some unobserved, but observable, physical reality. But in this case there is no further observable physical reality. The evidence for a transcendent dimension is simply the physical facts, perceived in a particular and disciplined fashion. It is the physical facts, seen as mediating something more than physical, something both attractive and demanding, something that gives greater significance to experience, yet something that cannot be separated off from experience as though it could exist and be discerned entirely on its own, without the experience.

I want to say that art is evidence, both strong and plentiful, for a transcendent dimension, for the existence of objective value and meaning. But the evidence will not be compelling for everyone. Some people will deny that it is evidence at all, especially if they think that all values are just subjective reactions to objective neutral facts. This disagreement cannot be theoretically resolved. It reveals a fundamental gulf between diverse ways of seeing human experience, and human knowledge of reality. There is no neutrally available evidence that will bridge that gulf.

This is, however, very different from saying that there is no evidence for objective meaning. It says that there is evidence for the existence of objective values in reality. But to accept that it is evidence (or reject it as evidence) requires a particular way of seeing the world, that cannot be conclusively, or even probably, established by argument or reasoning. Argument and reasoning are important, but they come later, as justifications of what we think we have seen or failed to see. People rightly try to give reasons for why their way of seeing things is illuminating and appropriate, and why other ways of seeing are misleading or too fanciful. But such arguments, though important and appropriate, come after the fact of seeing things in a certain light. They cannot be used as the basis for seeing things in that light.

Reflection on the experience of art suggests that there are fundamental ways of seeing, or **fundamental perspectives**, that are very different, and that cannot be resolved by simple appeal to sense-perception or by pure reasoning and logical argument. Evidence exists for each different fundamental perspective. It would be quite false to say that neither disputant had any evidence. Both have evidence, but neither considers the evidence the other produces to be important.

Seeing the existence of objective values and meanings in the arts has not necessarily much to do with God. There are many people who could accept objective value in the arts, but do not associate this at all with God. One of the best known is Iris Murdoch, who disliked God but argued forcefully for objective value in the arts. She is not alone. All I have said is that there is good evidence for objective and intrinsic values being part of the fabric of reality. I have called this evidence for the existence of a transcendent dimension to experience, something more than the physical, and yet communicated through certain physical forms.

Many people will reasonably say that seeing objective artistic values is not at all religious. There is even the possibility of a great deal of tension between artistic values and religious values. We see this in Plato, when he thinks poetry should be censored so that it should not express any immoral characters or actions. Religious authorities have sometimes prohibited certain kinds of music or artistic representation, because they are held to undermine moral standards.

Yet Plato also held that the apprehension of particular beautiful objects can lead to the apprehension of what he called 'the Good', one supreme spiritual (non-material) reality which in some way contains or is the source of all particular forms of goodness and beauty. Iris Murdoch was very sympathetic to this Platonic view of one supreme Good, though she did not call it God.[5] This may not be a very common or obvious way of seeing art in our own culture. Yet great art, or music, or drama, can evoke a sense of profound and transcendent meaning. It can be both intensely worth-while in itself, and it can evoke wider intuitions of a depth and significance which underlies and is expressed through various forms of sensory experience.

There is no 'proof' of one supreme spiritual reality from artistic experience. Art is too various and expressive of too many different perspectives on reality, not all of them positive or good by any means. What art does is to open a window onto depths of meaning and value in reality. In that sense it is evidence for the existence of objective values, values not merely constructed by human minds, values which have real existence, even though their reality can often only be brought into being by imaginative human creativity, and can only be discerned by a particular sort of sensitivity. Art is evidence for a spiritual dimension to human experience. This does not get you to God. But there is a problem for a materialist in saying that objective and intrinsic values exist, whether or not finite minds acknowledge them. In what sense do they exist? And how can they exist, if the universe is wholly composed only of purely physical elements?

It is at this point that the postulation of a non-human mind, or something mind-like, in which ideals of beauty exist, and which is able to make those ideals actual, or to inspire human minds to make them actual in the physical world, strikes many as reasonable and natural. If Spirit is thought of as supreme Beauty and as the source of all particular beautiful things, then evidence for objective values will be part of the evidence for Spirit. The evidence of footprints in the snow does not immediately lead you to a murderer, but it may be part of a cumulative body of evidence which can lead to the identification of a murderer. So thinking of Spirit as containing the ideas of all beautiful things, as instantiating supreme beauty in itself, and as shaping the physical world and inspiring human capacities to create and appreciate their own forms of beauty, provides a way of thinking of objective values as central to the nature of reality, and not just as some sort of unforeseen and fortuitous accident on the periphery of the material world. Spirit will be not a direct inference from intrinsic values. Spirit, in this respect, is more like a postulate which will make sense of a world in which intrinsic values have real existence. They also seem to have causal influence, even if that influence is rather indirect. They are ideals which become goals for human artistic activity and objects of human contemplation.

What we can say is that the postulate of Spirit would make the existence of objective values highly probable. By a simple law of logic, that entails that the existence of objective values raises the probability that there is such a reality as Spirit. Thus the existence of objective values is contributory evidence for the existence of supreme Spirit, even though on its own it is far from sufficient to compel belief in such a Spirit.

3.

----∞----

SPIRITUAL VALUES IN MORALITY

Morality as 'mediating evidence'

Just as art may be, but need not be, seen as evidence of transcendent meaning and value, so morality may be seen in a similar way. There are philosophers (like A. J. Ayer or J. L. Mackie) who insist that all moral values, all assessments of states as good or of acts as right or wrong, are purely subjective, with no foundation in objective reality. But, as Mackie admits, for most people a sense of right and wrong, or of goodness and badness, seems to express some truths which are not just about human states of mind.

For example, if I say, 'It is morally wrong to torture babies', I think most people would say that this really is wrong, even if some people find nothing wrong with such conduct. In saying it really is wrong, they mean that the statement 'it is wrong to torture babies' is true, and it is made true by some fact that is not a fact about any human mind. I do not care if some society thinks torturing babies is permissible. They are mistaken, and they have not seen an obvious truth.

The belief that there are moral truths cannot be proved, or demonstrated in a way that would compel every intelligent person to agree. But it is an immensely important and fundamental belief. You are a 'moral realist' if you think that there really is a moral pressure, a 'demand', upon moral agents to act in certain ways, or if you think that some states (like compassion or understanding) are really worth-while and good, whatever people think.

Is there evidence for moral realism? As in the case of art, the word 'evidence' does not seem quite right. There are no physical facts which will compel universal assent. That is because what is in question is whether there are any specifically moral facts, any features of reality that impose moral obligations on people. I suspect most people think there are, though probably most people do not ask this sort of theoretical question about the foundations of their morality.

The sort of moral fact I have in mind is this: suppose you come across a starving child by the road-side. You are hurrying to an important meeting, though you have food in your bag. Would you say that a perceptive person would have a sense of obligation to give the child some food, even if that causes some inconvenience? In other words, is what you experience in this situation just the occurrence of some neutral sense-experiences, to which you may or may not add some subjective feelings of pity or indifference? Or is part of what you experience a demand for action on your part, a demand which you may resist, though only at the cost of 'turning a blind eye' to the situation?

I believe that we experience such demands, that when we do so we are experiencing something real, not just having an inner feeling, and that it is possible to cultivate or to ignore such experiences, which will affect how we see them in future. In other words, people sometimes experience a moral depth to things, mediated in and through particular sensory observations. But people can make themselves more or less sensitive to such 'depth perceptions', and as they do so, they make themselves either more or less truly human. Becoming more truly human is being able to experience moral perceptions more clearly and fully. In other words, we experience what we make ourselves capable of experiencing. It is not a matter of just having or losing some inner feelings. It is a matter of learning to see more justly, or of losing that capacity and thereby losing our humanity.

The sense of transcendence

This is not evidence in a straightforward empirical sense. But it is evidence in a rather different sense. It is a fundamental way of seeing and being in the world. It expresses a fundamental perspective. It brings to attention specific features of human experience that give rise to a sense of transcendence, a sense that some sensory perceptions are most properly seen as mediators of objective 'demands' and 'ideals' that can call forth specific actions in the perceiver.

From a materialist (who says that reality consists of nothing but physical particles) or a crude empiricist (who says that reality consists of nothing but neutral, 'purely factual' sense-experiences) point of view, this will seem like nothing more than a projection of private feelings onto a morally neutral objective reality that has nothing like 'demands', 'ideals', or values in it at all. But are those points of view really more obvious and reasonable than the view that moral values exist in reality, even apart from human perceptions of them? Here, as the philosopher Wittgenstein said, we seem to reach bedrock. There is simply no neutral way of deciding what way of seeing and being in the world is more reasonable. There is no objective criterion of 'reasonableness' at this basic level.

The philosopher J. L. Mackie said that objective moral values are just too 'queer', too odd, to exist. But that sounds like a subjective and disputable opinion, if anything is! It is true that a reality with moral values in it, mediated through sense-perceptions, is very different from a reality with no moral values. If you accept that all knowledge begins with experience, all you can do is point to specific experiences the most natural interpretation of which is that they mediate moral values. I think the onus is on those who deny that interpretation to show why so many people are deluded. I do not think they have done this, or that they ever can. It is wholly implausible to say that many of the most saintly and intelligent people in the world have actually suffered delusions.

When we try to sort out what it is reasonable to believe about the world, we just have to seek the most consistent, coherent, and comprehensive set of concepts for interpreting human experience that we can. We seek an overall coherent explanation, and fit our particular experiences into that as best as we can. When we do that, the fact of the matter is that philosophers have come up with more than one candidate for being the best overall explanation, the best world view.

Some people are so impressed with the truly amazing success of the natural sciences in the last few hundred years that they think the best world view is a 'naturalistic' world view, one that explains everything in terms of the law-governed behaviour of physical particles. Having made that decision, they then have to fit things like moral values, consciousness, and intentions, into that world view.

Other people, like me, think that this naturalistic world view, fails the test of comprehensiveness. It simply ignores facts about values, and about private mental thoughts and feelings. I can see no evidence that would resolve this dispute. What you can and should do is bring out the considerations which cause you to prefer your own interpretation, and to think that it is true. This will involve pointing to specific experiences, and to the consequences that might follow from accepting or rejecting a specific interpretation of them.

Morality and transcendent value

Experiences which are central to a view of morality as mediating transcendent value are those of moral freedom and responsibility, of obligation, guilt, and the attraction of moral ideals. We need to give an account of these that seems coherent and plausible.[6] The moral realist should be able to provide a coherent account of a reality that includes both physical facts, and facts about sense experiences, and facts about moral values or ideals. It is not easy to do that, and perhaps all our accounts, realist and non-realist alike, will be rather provisional and weak at some points.

Believing in moral values does not entail believing in God. Philosophers like G. E. Moore believed in moral facts but not in God.[7] Nevertheless, moral facts can contribute towards a reasonable belief in God. That is because if there are moral demands and goals (ideals), they are obviously not parts either of a purely materialistic or of a purely sensory reality. They are, as Moore said, 'non-natural', not part of the world investigated by the methods of natural science and psychology. But how and where can such non-natural facts exist? For a determined materialist or a hard-line empiricist, moral facts are indeed too odd to exist. So if we believe in moral facts, that will be evidence for a non-materialist and non-empiricist view of reality. But that may still leave us in search of a coherent and plausible world view that can include facts about beauty and morality as well as facts about physical objects and sense-experiences.

There is one world view, however, which would have no trouble about finding a place for facts about beauty and goodness. It is a world view which makes finite reality a creation by a God who knows and intends that the physical world should exist. If God creates, presumably God does so for a reason, or with some purpose. It is natural to think that this purpose will become a moral goal for humans and other intelligent beings. It is something that they 'ought' to aim at, a good and worth-while state which they ought to seek. In this way the existence of God provides an intelligible home for the moral facts that seem so 'queer' to Mackie, because there is nowhere in his reality for them to be. For a theist, moral facts can very happily exist in the mind of God, who creates the universe precisely with a purpose in mind.

In a similar way, a creator God would fashion a world in which there exist many beautiful states, states the contemplation of which is worth-while for its own sake. Beauty would not just be in the eye of the beholder. It would be objectively in the mind of God, as a possibility which it is good for any finite mind to realise and enjoy. God not only provides a home for moral obligations and ideals. God also provides a home for those intrinsic values in the realisation and enjoyment of which true human happiness lies. Ultimately, God is that supreme Beauty in conscious union with which human lives find their greatest fulfilment. Ultimately, beauty and morality would be closely connected. For a theist, obedience to moral law is not simply doing your duty because it is right. Duty is transformed by love, love of the Good and Beautiful.

Of course you can believe in the objectivity of morals if you do not believe in a creator God. But such objectivity would make more sense if there was a spiritual (non-material) reality in which moral truths could exist, even if they were not known or accepted by human beings. Plato, who was certainly a moral realist, did not believe in one personal God, but in a rather more impersonal spiritual reality that he called 'the Good'. Aristotle did not believe in a creator God, but he thought that there was a 'God', a supreme and conscious spiritual reality, which acted as a sort of 'ideal attractor' for beings in the universe. This reality draws things towards itself because they are attracted to it. If you believe in the existence of a spiritual reality in any of these senses, this gives a special tone to morality. Morality will not be just a set of rules. It will be a path towards a goal or purpose set by a supremely desirable and beautiful being. If you think of the spiritual reality as God, you will want to help to realise God's purpose because of your love and desire for closer and deeper knowledge of God. You may believe that the purpose can be achieved, by God's help, and so you will not lose heart or despair that your moral efforts may be in vain. You may think that there is a special moral goal for your life, which you need to discover, and that will give your life a special and unique meaning.

There is something else of great importance about moral apprehension. Everyone sooner or later comes to realise that they fall short of the moral ideal for their lives. Every sensitive person knows that they are moral failures in many ways. The world is made much worse by thoughtless and selfish human actions. We play our part in this, and that can lead to guilt and despair. Sartre said that

'Hell is other people'. But we also know that we can make our own lives Hell. So a sensitivity to moral perception can lead to a sense that we are moral failures, and to a felt need for some form of forgiveness or reconciliation.

If you think of a God who is not a ruthless judge, but who is a compassionate and loving observer of the human drama, that can lead to a hope that forgiveness and reconciliation is possible. Perhaps a power greater than our own can make possible what is impossible for us. In that way a profound moral sense can lead to a sense of what Matthew Arnold (who did not believe in God in any conventional sense) called 'a power not ourselves which makes for righteousness'. In other religious traditions which do not speak of God, but which do think that reality has a spiritual basis (like Buddhism), it can lead to reliance on a compassionate Buddha and to a turning from a life of selfish desire towards a life of greater mindfulness and universal compassion.

Thus the sense of morality can carry with it a sense of objective moral demand, personal moral failure, and the compassionate presence of a power that can help us achieve a true moral goal. This is a fundamental perspective on morality. Not everyone shares that perspective. For some people, morality is little more than a set of restrictions on personal freedom which may be necessary to hold society together, but is otherwise an unnecessary burden on human life. The fundamental decision about what morality really is, and what its force and importance is, is not one that can be made by reason alone. It depends upon our deepest perceptions of the nature of human existence and of reality.

So evidence for a spiritual dimension of existence exists, if we see moral experience as mediating transcendent value and moral purpose. Nothing can make us see it that way. This is evidence that only exists within one fundamental perspective. But those who see it that way may think that no one can evade the sense, however fleetingly, that this transcendent perspective is authentic and vitally important to human existence.

I am not saying that everyone has to believe in objective moral facts. I am not saying that if you do believe in moral facts, you have to believe in God. I am saying that belief in objective moral facts is entirely reasonable and entirely natural. If God exists, moral facts will have a natural and intelligible place in reality. That makes moral experience evidence for God, as well as for some rather different, non-theistic but definitely non-materialist, views. Such evidence will remain essentially contestable and its interpretation will remain controversial, as any evidence is at this level. It is still evidence, however, and will form part of a cumulative case for the reality of a spiritual realm of being.

When I say that the evidence is contestable, I do not mean that there is nothing to choose between different beliefs, or that they are all equally acceptable. After all, only one of two or more conflicting beliefs can be correct. What I mean is that there is no neutral way of convincing all intelligent and informed disputants which is the right one. The best way of understanding this is to recognise that people have different fundamental perspectives, and what people are prepared to count as good evidence will largely depend upon what that perspective is.

If we are asked to justify our perspective, we may well just have to point to the practical consequences we believe it has, and to the overall coherence and comprehensiveness to which we think it gives rise. Those things are evidence; but they are not like finding foot-prints in the snow, which everyone can see and agree about. The notions of both 'experience' and of 'evidence' are broader and more complex than that. They allow for fundamentally different perspectives. The beginning of wisdom in philosophy is to accept this as a fact, and to learn how to present your own perspective reasonably in the light of it.

4.

SPIRITUAL VALUES IN PHILOSOPHY

Interpreting reality

I have argued that it is too crude a view of 'experience' to say that it just consists in the occurrence of bare and uninterpreted sense-experiences. I have suggested that feelings can be a form of apprehension, which give access to features of reality that you might otherwise miss. Artistic and moral insights are naturally seen as pointing to objective and 'non-natural' features of reality which are mediated in and through sense-impressions.

Experience cannot be reduced just to the occurrence of sense-experiences. In fact those sense-experiences would not even give rise to knowledge unless there were intellectual interpretations which organise and integrate our very diverse sense-impressions. We do not just have sense-impressions. We interpret them as impressions of an externally existing world of objects in three dimensional space, having causal relations with one another, and obeying regular laws of nature. Without that interpretation, our sense-impressions would not even make sense. As the philosopher Immanuel Kant said, sense-impressions without concepts are 'blind', and concepts without sense-impressions are 'empty'.[8] We need a set of concepts, of thoughts, to interpret our sense-impressions so that we can understand them.

The mind is not merely passive, receiving sense-impressions onto a blank sheet of paper. The mind is active from the first, uniting different sense-impressions of sight, sound, and touch into one unitary experience, uniting past experiences to present ones so that we have one unique continuing series of experiences, and integrating our impressions so that they give us information about an external world.

Part of the job of philosophy is to examine these mental activities of interpretation, and try to say what they tell us about the external world, and how they do it. It is fairly widely agreed among philosophers (but not universally agreed; that rarely happens in philosophy) that there are certain features needed to give a good interpretation of experience. First, good interpretations should be **simple** and elegant. Second, they should give a **consistent** view that avoids self-contradictions and does not conflict with other well-established knowledge. Third, they should be **comprehensive**, taking into account as many different aspects of experience as possible. Fourth, they should provide some sort of **integrated** unity among experiences, rather than leaving a disconnected set of unrelated data. And fifth, they should be **fruitful**, having practical consequences that are helpful in enabling humans to live well.

Materialism and Idealism

In the history of philosophy, there have been many general interpretations of experience (these are sometimes called systems of metaphysics, though some prefer to call them systems of ontology – not a difference I want to explore here). Two of the most fundamental, which seem to be in complete opposition to each other, are materialism and idealism. Historically, there have not been many materialists among philosophers. Generally speaking, materialists hold that everything that exists consists of matter. There are no spiritual realities, and matter probably consists of elementary particles governed by laws of nature. Those particles get into very complicated patterns, and when they are complicated enough they form human beings. Human consciousness, feeling, and thought are nothing but a complicated arrangement of material particles.

Idealists, on the other hand, think that matter could not exist without mind or consciousness (what I have called Spirit). Material things exist, but they exist in order to express the nature of Spirit in some way. So Spirit is fundamentally real, and matter is dependent on Spirit.

Idealism often begins with the observation that human experience, human feelings and thoughts, exist and are not reducible to purely material, unconscious, unfeeling, unthinking, objects or any combination of such objects. Some intelligible place has to be found for feelings and thoughts in our account of reality.

The next step towards Idealism is to say that all our knowledge of the physical world is built up from conscious experiences, and the very idea of an objectively existing physical world is a postulate which we accept because it makes good sense of our experiences. The world as we experience it is largely mind-constructed, since such experienced properties as colour, sound, solidity, and taste do not exist in the reality which produces these experiences in us when that reality is observed by us. The world as we experience it is not the world as it exists apart from our observations. We have no access to such a non-experienced world, except as a postulated reality to explain the occurrence of our various experiences. The 'physical world' is a postulated explanatory framework which abstracts certain properties (physical properties) from our experience and thinks of them as objectively existing. There is little other reason, however, for thinking that the physical world as we experience it is independently real. So mind is the basis for the world as we experience it.

A third step to Idealism is to suggest that, just as mind is the basis of the world as we observe it, so mind is the basis of unobserved reality, which contains values, intelligibility, and beauty as well as physical facts. Just as our minds create an experienced reality, so there is a cosmic mind which creates a reality which contains the objective values which we can appreciate in our own experience. This step reverses the materialist hypothesis, and proposes that value and experience are fundamental to reality, while the physical is the instrumental vehicle which is needed to generate and make specific experienced values real. It is not the physical which generates (without knowing or desiring it) consciousness of values. It is a conscious valuing mind which generates the physical as a means to realising new sorts of experienced values.

Though they do not always realise it, people who believe in God are idealists, in this sense. So they are committed to a particular philosophical view. I believe that when they realise that, belief in God immediately becomes much more rational and defensible. It is, after all, not just adding a superfluous and additional entity to the world, which is quite in order as it is. It is agreeing with one of the major interpretations of reality that classical philosophers have accepted.[9] One main source of evidence for God lies in the success of idealism as a philosophy.

Many philosophers would dispute, of course, that idealism is a successful philosophy. These days some philosophers are scientific materialists, even though historically there have not been many major philosophers who are materialists. They think that physical science provides one very simple and elegant interpretation of experience. It is a unitary interpretation, reducing all experience to just one level of explanation. It does not involve any 'spooky' or arbitrary entities (like God) which might interfere with the unity of nature. And it is very fruitful, having transformed our view of nature and enabled us to improve standards of health and means of communication enormously. There is a lot to be said for it.

So there is evidence for materialism. The postulated laws of nature seem to work, and the success of the sciences is indisputable. But the real attraction of materialism lies in its theoretical simplicity and unity. Ultimately, there are just a few simple laws of nature, and there is no need to introduce arbitrary entities like minds or God, which just complicate life and have no real explanatory value.

The best evidence for materialism is not sense-experience. In fact sense-experience is a major problem for materialists. Nobody knows how the fundamental laws of physics give rise to conscious experience, and the experienced world of three-dimensional solid objects seems to be very different from the world some physicists talk about, which has eleven dimensions and nothing really solid in it! Even time, according to many physicists, is an illusion, as it does not really 'flow' at all, but is it is all there at once. Yet in experience time does seem to flow, and one thing happens after another. The world you experience looks very different from the world physics tells you about. To put it bluntly, materialists prefer an elegant theory to sense-experience, and have to explain human experience away as just a set of appearances that are not objectively real. The really strong evidence for materialism is the elegance and integrating power of scientific explanation.

Suppose, however, that you sympathise with the drive to find simplicity, consistency, comprehensiveness, integration and fruitfulness in your interpretation of experience. You also sympathise with the suspicion that sense-impressions are appearances of a deeper underlying objective reality. But you want to find a place for the sense of meaning and beauty that great art and many features of the natural world can give, and for the sense of demand and attraction that seems to you to be inherent in morality. In other words, you want to find a coherent place for experiences and for objective values as well as neutral 'facts' in the fabric of reality. Then Idealism may seem to provide a more comprehensive and coherent view of reality.

The idea of a creator

The Idealist option, which has been espoused in slightly different ways by Plato, Aristotle, Aquinas, Descartes, Leibniz, Spinoza, Kant, Hegel, Berkeley, and many other – and in fact by most – major philosophers, is that the ultimate reality which underlies the sensorily experienced world is a mind-like reality of supreme value. The most famous of all philosophers, Plato, did not think that this reality created the universe. He thought the universe of matter just always existed alongside the supreme value, the Good. There were traces or faint images of the Good in the material universe. In that sense, you might say there was 'evidence' for the existence of the Good in the universe. But the universe was not created. It was just there.

When Anselm set out to define a being that he called God, however, he defined it as the most perfect possible (or 'the greatest conceivable') being. That, he thought, implies that the Supreme Spirit, God, creates the universe. If a being is the most perfect possible being, it will be more powerful than any other being. And it can only guarantee this if it is the cause of every other being that exists. God will be the one and only cause of every being that exists, except itself. God will be 'the First Cause'. Most philosophers in the West since that time have continued to call this being God. It may not be very like the God of the Bible, or the one that many religious people worship. To assert that Anselm's God was like the Biblical God would need a good deal of argument that I am not going to discuss. I just want to consider, from a philosophical point of view, what it would mean to think that the supreme Spirit, for which I will use the word God, as Anselm did, created the universe.

It does not mean that God existed before the universe, and set it going at some point in time. It means that the whole universe, from beginning to end (if it has a beginning and end, as most scientists think it has), depends upon God for its existence. Without God, it would not exist at all. God does not just set the universe going at the beginning ('light the blue touch paper', as Stephen Hawking has put it). God has to keep the universe in existence at every moment. God is the spiritual reality without which no physical reality could exist at all, even for one second. Creation is not the beginning of the universe. It is the dependence of the physical universe at every time and place upon a non-physical reality. Without Spirit there would be no matter.

There is something else to creation. God is not just the 'First Cause'. God generates the universe by knowing and intending it. Creation is not just a blind emergence from nothing, which happens without anybody knowing about it, or without any purpose. If the universe is created, it has a purpose. That means that something like a mind (a knowing and acting being) knew what it was doing, and intended to make the whole universe exist.

So as well as thinking of God as the supreme value, those who postulate creation must think of God as something like a mind (but very different from any human mind) which knows all possible universes that could ever exist, and chooses to make one (or more) of them exist, for a purpose. Since the best and most rational (the most perfect) minds choose things because they think such things are worth-while or good, God will choose universes for the sake of their goodness. In this sense, the purpose of God in creating the universe is bound to be good.

Physics does not deal with creation by a God, because creation is a purposive action by a purely spiritual being. Physics is about physical realities, and so cannot really discover anything by observation and experiment about Spirit or about what might be going on in the mind of God. But some physical facts are relevant to deciding whether or not a spiritual reality exists and has effects on the physical world. For instance, if that spiritual reality does have spiritual purposes for the universe, that must make some difference to the nature of the universe. The universe must have some signs of purpose in it somewhere.

It may be thought that this is a purely scientific question, but it is not. You can have all the known physical facts about the universe, and still not be sure whether there are purposes in it or not. There is no observable purposer, and it is not clear whether processes are really goal-directed, or whether mechanical principles have just produced the appearance of purpose. Questions of value are also involved (since a purpose is a process aimed at some state of value). One will have to ask whether the universe really shows evidence of great value, whether it is worth-while, and whether a basically good creator could have chosen it. Such questions are not value-neutral, and they cannot be settled conclusively by appeal to purely empirical evidence or elegant scientific theories. Answers depend upon the values that enquirers themselves accept or think they perceive. So there are many questions about the best overall interpretation of cosmic processes to be addressed, and these are philosophical questions, though of course they require a good knowledge of all relevant scientific facts.

Looking for evidence of cosmic purpose will be very different from looking for evidence that some rare physical animal exists somewhere in the universe. But there are certainly considerations that count for or against the existence of purpose. I will try to show that there is evidence for cosmic purpose and for the existence of a cosmic mind which formulates that purpose. I accept, however, that the evidence is not of the sort that will convince everyone, and that different thinkers will evaluate the strength of the evidence differently. That fact will nevertheless help to make my main point, which is that evidence does exist, but that there is no way of conclusively establishing a conclusion to everyone's satisfaction. Therefore it is false to say that there is no evidence for cosmic purpose. And it is false to say that belief in a cosmic mind which formulates such a purpose is somehow less rational than disbelief or agnosticism about such a mind.

5.

PURPOSE AND EVIL

The idea of cosmic purpose

One reason that some philosophers are not happy with the idea of a God or cosmic mind who creates the universe for a purpose is that they think God must be a being external to the universe who intervenes in it from outside. This threatens the unity and integrity of nature. So philosophers like Thomas Nagel think that while there might be some sense of purpose in the universe, that purpose should not be associated with the action of a God.

I think the word 'intervention' has done a great deal of harm here. You do not have to think of God as a being who interferes in the clockwork of the universe to adjust the works from time to time. You could think of God as the deepest reality of the universe. The claim is that the physical universe is not complete on its own. It is grounded in supra-cosmic laws and energies, which in turn are grounded in ultimate mind, the mind of God. So God does not have to intervene in a closed universe. God is the reality within which the physical universe exists, and without which the universe would not exist at all. Whatever happens is an expression of aspects of the mind of God. That is not something foreign to the universe; it is the deepest nature of the universe. How can its own deepest nature 'intervene' in what is an expression of that nature?

You need to get away from the idea that there is a closed set of physical laws, which do not quite manage to produce life and mind and reason by themselves, so that God has to step into keep re-directing things to get the results God wants (this is what is sometimes called the 'Intelligent Design' hypothesis, and it is a hypothesis which most philosophers reject). There are two things wrong with this picture – first, that the laws are a closed system which is entirely self-maintaining, and second, that God needs to step in occasionally to adjust the system when it is not doing quite what God wants.

Think of the universe, instead, as a growing and developing system which gradually unfolds possibilities which have been present in it from the first, but become actual through a long process of development. As time goes by, the structures in the universe get more complex, and organise themselves into highly integrated patterns. This evolving universe, for a quantum physicist, does not run down boringly predetermined tram-lines. Stephen Hawking suggests that 'given the initial state of a system, nature determines its future state through a process that is fundamentally uncertain' (*The Grand Design*, p. 92).[10] This means that there are many possible futures at every stage of the universe's existence. It is not just that we don't and can't know the future. That future is objectively uncertain, not yet fixed even by God. Yet there seems to be a direction of unfolding, from simpler to more complex, from unconscious to more conscious, from regular and repetitive to new and creative. There is a probabilistic direction to things, but a lot of open-ness in the process. A widely accepted modern scientific view of the universe is that it is open (has many possible futures), emergent (generates new properties as it evolves more complex and integrated structures), and goal-directed, directed towards the emergence of consciousness, intelligence, and reason.

How does the universe move in that direction? Laws of physics are often seen as causal laws which have no particular goal or purpose. But there might be deeper laws of development, laws which make the universe move towards a goal, partly (and increasingly, as organisms get more complex and conscious) by the creative and self-shaped decisions of sentient beings which emerge as intrinsic parts of the universe. Such laws would not be interventions in a simpler set of causal laws. They would be the deepest laws of nature itself. The presence of God as ultimate mind, as the all-inclusive spiritual boundary of the physical universe, would exercise a continuing influence on how the laws of physics operate. The biologist Arthur Peacocke called this a 'whole-part' influence.[11] The whole is not just the addition of all the actions of its parts. It exercises a shaping influence on those parts, influencing, but not wholly determining, how the parts of the whole behave.

In a way, this is just saying that the way parts behave on their own is very different from the way they behave when they become part of a more complex organised structure. Somehow the organisation itself modifies the behaviour of the parts, giving them a function within the whole. An example of this would be the development of cells in a human body. Each human starts as a blastocyst, a bundle of identical cells. As an embryo develops, the cells take on different functions. Some become parts of fingers, some become parts of intestines, and some become parts of brains. Cells which all begin as identical develop very different functions, depending upon where in the growing organism they are situated. In some way the pattern of the whole is influencing the behaviour of its parts, the individual cells which make up the body. Such influence is not an intervention; it can be seen as a non-determining tendency which modifies the behaviour of its parts. The parts build up into a complex society, and the developing structure of that society changes the way the parts behave.

Since that tendency is inherent in the nature of things from their origin, the universe is from its first physical beginnings oriented towards realising those ideas. They are present as goals inherent in the genesis of the universe itself. This gives the universe an inherently purposive character. The universe has the developing structure it has in order that it might realise such values as intelligence and creative freedom. If that is the case, it seems that there would have to be something like a mind with ideas of future possibilities, awareness of the values of those possibilities, and causal power to bring some of them about, even before there is any complex physical stuff at all.

This in turn would entail that mind cannot just be a sort of 'inner side' of matter, developing gradually along with matter. It has to be able to direct matter, from the beginning, to its goal – the existence of communities of free conscious intelligent agents. That mind may still find its natural and proper, perhaps even inevitable, expression in the existence of a physical universe. But mind will have priority over matter. It can reasonably be called God, the creator of the universe.

Such an idea is at the heart of the way that Aristotle thought of the natural world. He saw the universe as 'attracted' towards an ideal goal, which existed trans-temporally and necessarily. Aristotle did not believe the physical universe was created, or brought into being by God on purpose. But he did think there was a God, and that God does exert a causal and purposive influence on the universe.

One reason why Aristotle may have hesitated to say that the universe is intentionally created by God is because of the amount of seeming 'wastefulness' and suffering in the world. Millions of species have become extinct, millions of stars and planets have exploded and died. Millions of genetic defects have caused pain and suffering at least to the higher animals. How could a mind which designs the universe in order to realise values allow that to happen?

In his book, *Mind and Cosmos*, the philosopher Thomas Nagel[12] argues that, if mind and reason are distinctive and irreducible features of the universe, there must be some form of explanation that sees them as more than accidental by-products of the basic laws of nature. In some way their possibility and development must be included in the laws of nature. There must, he argues, be some sort of teleology, purposiveness, in the basic laws of nature, which makes the emergence of minds implicit already in the laws governing the origin of the physical universe. Many physicists, including for instance Paul Davies and Freeman Dyson, are sympathetic to this idea. Paul Davies says, 'The existence of mind in some organism on some planet in the universe is surely a fact of fundamental significance. Through conscious beings the universe has generated self-awareness. This can be no trivial detail, no minor byproduct of mindless, purposeless forces. We are truly meant to be here' (*The Mind of God*, Simon and Schuster, 1992, p. 242).[13]

Mind and value, Nagel suggests, are closely, perhaps essentially, connected. Minds will, if they can, choose what seems to them to be of value. Value only actually exists if some mind recognises and appreciates it as value. Thus there will be no actually existing values without minds, and since minds are essentially active in thought and action, they will think and act for the sake of values. Since life, mind, and value emerge together, Nagel suggests that what might explain the appearance of life in the universe is that life brings value into the world. 'There is life because life is a necessary condition of value' (p. 123). This is the axiological principle (from the Greek word *axia,* which means 'value'). The universe exists because it realises distinctive sorts of values. Though Nagel does not believe in God, because of the religious associations of that word, which he does not like, this does sound very like an argument for God, or at least like a way of seeing the universe in the light of the priority of mind and value. For only a cosmic mind could envisage those values, and generate a universe from which they would emerge. The emergence of those values in some form would be inevitable. But the particular form they take might depend upon the interactions of many partly self-organising entities in the universe (including the ones we know most about, human beings).

Is purpose compatible with evil?

Nagel is an atheist. He has no feeling for God, and does not like God. He thinks that if there were a God, the teleological process would be benign or 'optimistic'. But it is not, because it gives rise to both good and evil. So he thinks the purposive tendency might be just immanent in the natural universe itself, as 'a tendency toward the proliferation of complex forms' (p. 122). However, that does not seem to be enough for what he really wants. Complexity alone does not entail either value or disvalue. You probably cannot have value in the physical universe without considerable complexity. That is because the actual existence of value depends upon the existence of a consciousness that recognises that value, and consciousness, at least of a human sort, depends upon the considerable physical complexity of a brain. But it is not the complexity of the brain that is important. It is the recognition of value which the brain makes possible. If there is a purposive tendency in the universe, it is unlikely to be just towards complexity for its own sake. There is no value in that. A purposive process must tend towards something of value, it must aim at value. Nagel's problem is: how can we see the cosmic process as purposive, if there is so much disvalue, so much evil, in the cosmos? That is one of the most basic and difficult problems of philosophy.

A way, perhaps the only acceptable way, of accounting for the disvalues that exist in a purposive universe is that the sort of teleology that exists in this universe is a tendency to realise values of a sort from which some disvalues are inseparable. If this is true, the process may properly be called ultimately benign and optimistic, because it will be consciously aimed at values. Many values of a very great and distinctive nature will be fully realised only in a process like this. But this process also inevitably produces evils. These evils are not consciously aimed at, but they cannot be wholly eliminated without destroying the process. They are necessary features of a universe which produces values of this distinctive sort. Or, to be more precise, these values cannot exist unless it is necessarily true that some disvalues of a certain type must exist, and that other disvalues may possibly come to exist as well, depending largely upon what decisions free creatures make.

As a matter of fact, Stephen Hawking gives one of the best explanations for why the process should be like that. He says, 'The laws of nature form a system that is extremely fine-tuned, and very little in physical law can be altered without destroying the possibility of the development of life as we know it' (GD, p. 205).

The 'fine-tuning' argument is one of the best known discoveries in modern science. I will not rehearse it here, as it can be found in many recent books on popular science.[14] It depends on the fact that many basic laws and the values of forces like gravity and electric charge have to be almost exactly what they are to produce a universe which is stable enough to develop carbon-based life-forms like us. Very slight changes in the nuclear force or the electric force would destroy even the possibility of intelligent life like ours.

This is a remarkable fact, about which there is very little disagreement among scientists (though there are many disagreements about exactly what it implies). One thing it does seem to entail is that we, as the specific beings we are, could not exist in any universe with different laws and forces. We belong in this universe, and if we are going to exist at all, we just have to exist in this universe, with its particular laws. So if we sometimes wish we existed in a better universe, this argument reminds us that, while other beings might exist in better universes, we could not. We just have to put up with this one.

The special sorts of values that we produce – values, perhaps, like love, the creation of beautiful things, overcoming obstacles to achieve difficult and worth-while tasks, setting out on a personal journey to find difficult but worth-while goals of our own choosing, and seeking, with effort and patience, to understand the laws of nature – could not even exist if we did not live in a world where lack of love, ugliness, failures, and misunderstandings were also possible, probably even inevitable to some extent.

Some religious people think that a perfect God would never create anything evil, so that everything that happened would always be good. If that was true, then God would never have created us! As Albert Einstein once asked, 'Did God have any choice when he created the universe?' Well, maybe God need not have created us. But if God wanted to create us, with all our faults and failings, maybe God had not much choice about the basic laws and forces that would make up our universe.

Evil and omnipotence

It is sometimes said that if God is all-powerful, he must be powerful enough to be able to change the laws of nature and still create humans. But that is not obvious. Nobody who thinks about it believes that God can do absolutely anything. God cannot, for instance, commit suicide, or do anything evil just for fun, or turn himself completely into a frog. There are things even the most powerful possible being cannot do.

If God is the most powerful possible being, then God cannot logically become weak. If God knows everything, then he cannot become ignorant. If God is supremely valuable, then he cannot become unhappy or evil. God, to put it in traditional philosophical terms, is at least in some major respects, necessarily what God is – supremely powerful, knowing, and good. In these respects, God is necessarily what God is; there is no alternative.

So we have to admit that even the most powerful possible God is limited (but not in a bad way) by the necessities of the divine nature. We also have to admit that we do not know what these necessities are. It seems likely, for example, that in a perfect being divine omnipotence will be limited by divine goodness. Then God will not be able directly to intend some evil things – there will be some things God cannot do. And there will be some things that God cannot help doing – for instance, if God creates anything, God will necessarily intend to create good things. But some good things may only be able to exist in a universe that also contains bad things. For all we know, God may necessarily create many forms of overwhelming goodness, many of which will involve some bad things. If this is so, God may necessarily generate some states (states of suffering, for instance) that God does not consciously intend. Necessity, for reasons unknown in detail by us, may decree that some destructive or obstructive elements present in the divine mind must become actualised. They need not be positively intended by God, though they will still arise from God, and they may be implied by a sort of universe, with great and otherwise unobtainable good things in it, that God does intend (do not forget that when I talk about God, I am talking about a cosmic mind. What I am asking is whether this could, logically speaking, be a mind that intends to produce good, and yet somehow, without intending it, produces lots of evil and suffering. I am arguing, in effect, that it could be).

In a similar way, divine power could well be limited by divine freedom. If God is able to generate finite creatures who can make radically free decisions, then perhaps even God would not know what exactly they would decide. Then God would not know in advance just how God would respond to their free decisions. As a result, God's power would be limited by having to allow for things happening that God did not intend or even know about in advance.

So although it may seem that a perfect being would be unlimitedly powerful, that may not be true. If a perfect being is a being who is perfect in goodness, who allows creatures real creative freedom, and who thinks it good, or even finds it necessary, to create a great many different forms of goodness, there may be real limits – not external constraints, but inherent in the divine being itself - on divine power. Perhaps we should say, not that God has absolutely unlimited power, but rather that God will have the greatest power that is compatible with the divine nature, including whatever in the divine nature is necessarily what it is. That is why I am prepared to modify Anselm's postulate that God is greater (more valuable) than any other being that could be conceived (by us). My point is that we might *think* we can imagine an absolutely all-powerful being who could create humans without creating any evil. But we might be wrong. There might be things that are necessary even in the most valuable being who could possibly exist, but we might well not know what they are. So maybe we should say that God is the most valuable being that could possibly exist, but admit (as Anselm himself does elsewhere) that our imaginations are not very good at knowing what exactly this will be.

We know very little about the necessities and interconnections of the physical world. What we call waste could be a consequence of the creative spontaneity and experimentation of the biosphere.

That biosphere might generate, without simply determining, many partly self-organising complex forms, which will realise many diverse sorts of value that could not otherwise have existed. Sometimes it is complained that it should not have taken billions of years just to produce us. But billions of years of interstellar space is not a waste, as it has its own beauty and energy, in which a conscious God could delight – and, of course, before sentient life-forms exist, it contains no suffering, so there is no problem of evil. And we humans are surely not the final goal of this universe, though our intelligence, freedom, and capacity for loving relationships, are worthy of being at least small parts of such a final goal.

Suffering is real, and it is undesirable by any rational being, at least it is undesirable for its own sake. But it could be a consequence of the increasing sensitivity of complex organisms to their environment, and also of the mistreatment of many life-forms by human carelessness or malevolence. It may also be an unavoidable by-product of the working of the laws of nature, the general character of which is to bring new forms of being out of vast and potentially destructive forces.

It is very hard not to see the almost fourteen billion year process of the universe from the Big Bang – with no complexity, no perceived values, and no organisation – to human life on the planet earth – with many conscious beings learning to understand the universe and to control parts of it – as other than a long progress towards consciousness, reason, and value. It looks as though the universe is engaged in a process of coming to understand itself and beginning to control the future at least of parts of itself. Such values are intelligible goals of activity. In other words, there is evidence of purpose in the universe, a purpose which is attained through creative risk, suffering, and striving against adversity. It looks as if the universe moves purposefully, through hardship and unrelenting endeavour, towards the generation of understanding, reasoning, and moral responsibility.

We may think of a 'universe' as an inter-related set of states of affairs, connected in complex causal ways, which develops as an organic totality within which each event affects all other events in sometimes subtle, sometimes dramatic, ways. If some universes are, as I have suggested, open, emergent, and goal-directed, then in selecting such a universe, a cosmic intelligence would select a developing system that was not wholly under his its control. The system would combine chance ('open-ness'), necessity (causal interconnectedness and regularity), purpose (orientation to good), and emergently free finite choices ('autonomy'), in ways which necessarily limit the exercise of divine determining power. This may be such a universe, and in it the realisation of distinctive values would co-exist with the existence of much disvalue – none of which is chosen by God for its own sake, though God is the ultimate cause of it nonetheless.

Most views which posit the existence of a creator God would add that, though suffering may be an inevitable part of this universe, a being which creates for the sake of good would want to ensure that good was fulfilled and evil finally defeated. It would be safe to assume that all the valued states this universe produces, if they are all known by God, would be retained in the mind of God, while all the disvalues of the world would be mitigated in the mind of God by being placed in a wider context of fulfilled goodness. In that case, created persons could, after death in this universe, share in the mind of God in some appropriate way. Then they could fulfil the natures which have been shaped in this universe, moving on to experience new forms of goodness, free from the sufferings which have been part of their experience as creatively and morally free beings in this universe. If that is the case, and if they could not have existed at all as the precise persons they are without having being born in this universe, then that would considerably strengthen the case for saying that this universe, with all its evil, could be created by a good God.

From a philosophical point of view, this requires that persons in this universe could go on to exist in a different universe or form of being, not subject to the physical laws of this universe. Idealists, who believe that minds are not necessarily physical, though they are properly embodied in some bodily form, are likely to hold that the same minds could be embodied in different 'bodily' forms. If so, a life beyond physical death is logically possible, and in it the good could overwhelmingly outweigh and annihilate evil for every personal being. In this way, it could be that created reality (of which this physical universe is only part) has a purpose which will inevitably be achieved, and which makes the existence of this universe overwhelmingly good. Yet for the final realisation of that purpose, much hardship, destruction, and suffering must be endured by sentient beings. That suffering would, on such a view, be transformed by being included and given wider meaning within an experience of the total history of the arduous self-unfolding of a universe whose destiny is final union with the supreme Good.

6.

---◆◇◆---

PHILOSOPHICAL IDEALISM

Cosmic evolution and purpose

The purpose of the universe, though it obviously could not exist without this universe, can perhaps only be fully realised beyond the universe itself, in a form that will fully realise the values and annihilate the disvalues that have been generated in the universe. This is a possibility upon which many religions build, and perhaps it actuality depends upon the truth of specifically religious considerations.

But even without such a life beyond death, an axiological or purposive account of the existence of the universe would provide an explanation of why it exists in the way it does. The blunt assertion that the universe just happens to exist, and that is that, does not satisfy many scientists. Stephen Hawking, for example, says, 'Our universe and its laws appear to have a design that both is tailor-made to support us and, if we are to exist, leaves little room for alteration' (p. 207). Like the Astronomer-Royal, Martin Rees (also an agnostic about God), Hawking thinks the appeal to pure chance is just giving up on the basis of science, which is an unrelenting search for reasons, not accidents.

It certainly seems that the existence of a God who desired to create certain sorts of values, and who also desired that finite intelligences would be creatively free and self-shaping to a large extent, would provide an explanation of why a universe like this exists. In that sense scientific findings that support fine-tuning and the interconnected or holistic nature of physical reality provide good evidence for God, even if not any sort of conclusive proof.

There are many features of the universe that seem so amazingly complex and finely adjusted that the mind almost inevitably thinks that something more than pure chance is at stake. It is often said that the generalised Darwinian mechanisms of random mutation and competitive selection can fully account for those features. But assertions of randomness need to be treated with care. Mutations are not in fact totally random. They are caused by the operation of physical laws, and mutations have to be not too great and not too small, they have to be exactly right, if they are to give rise to evolutionary development. There is competition in evolution, but there is also a great deal of co-operation and symbiosis needed if complex organisms are to develop.

It is a brilliant Darwinian insight that the production of many variants and a process of competitive ('natural') selection can produce new and 'improved' sorts of complex organisms. But it is still an extraordinary fact that some of those variations produce increasingly complex integrated organic systems, and that selection has led to consciousness and increased intelligence and the sense of moral freedom. In other words, the existence of the evolutionary process itself seems to stand in need of explanation. Randomness in the sense of pure chance, and selection in the sense of a purely fortuitous survival of some organisms, does not seem enough to account for the development of human brains from primitive one-celled bacteria-like entities. There are so many ways in which pure chance could have led only to organic disintegration, and the struggle for existence could have led to the mutual extinction of all forms of life. That there should have been a cumulative increase of complexity of just the sort needed to lead to the existence of intelligent life is so improbable, given the huge number of alternative possibilities, that it seems much too weak to attribute it to pure chance. Such an explanation ('Random mutation and natural selection did it') is, after all, so vague and incomplete in detail that it is not much better than saying, 'God did it' – and everyone agrees that is not a satisfactory explanation!

It is incredible that the initial state of the universe at the Big Bang was just right to produce fundamental particles like strings, quarks, electrons, protons, and the other elements of the 'particle zoo', whose forces are synchronised in exactly the right way to form fairly stable atoms. These in turn combine to form the elements of chemistry, which form into stars and planets. Even more amazingly, long combinations of atoms, molecules, form the self-replicating structures of RNA and DNA. As the head of the human genome project, Francis Collins,[15] has said, the structure of DNA, with its three billion elements arranged in a precise coding-sequence, is not just a complex combination of chemicals. The important thing about it is that it forms a code, a complex string of information, which is used to construct proteins, which form organic bodies.

Piling one amazing process on another, organic bodies become more complex and integrated, forming central nervous systems and brains. Brains are extremely complex networks of 10 billion neurons, connected in thousands of ways, and giving rise to conscious experiences and reactions. Then, in the higher primates, and perhaps only in humans, the capacity for abstract thought and reasoning emerges from this billion year process of increasing integration and organisation.

It certainly seems incredible. It *could* have all happened by chance, but if there was an intelligence which designed and oversaw the process, the occurrence of the process would be hugely more probable. If God is the best hypothesis on other grounds (of simplicity, coherence, and fruitfulness, for example), that might show that the existence of God is more probable than any alternative known to us. And that is evidence.

Probability is a very tricky subject, and there is little agreement on how to assess the probability of humans having evolved simply by undirected changes in the genetic code and a process of weeding out those who did not replicate successfully (the two main Darwinian mechanisms of evolution). Biologists sometimes say that they can prove evolution was undirected or random. That is not true. What they have shown at best is that, as far as we can see, the evolutionary process could have come about without intelligent direction. It is not totally impossible, though most biologists admit that it is extremely improbable. The extremely improbable can happen, but the fact that it can happen does not show that it did happen. If the whole process would be more probable on the assumption of an intelligent creator, that is certainly good evidence for such a creator. It should not be simply discounted as an irrational or arbitrary hypothesis.

Alternatives to God

If there is purpose, does there have to be a purposer? Some mind envisaging a goal of value, and then selecting a set of procedures for the sake of obtaining that goal? Sometimes the mathematician John Conway's 'Game of Life', which he designed to produce interesting forms by using a very simple starting point and a few simple rules of movement, is used to show that organised complexity can emerge on its own from very simple starting-points. But in fact it needed someone with great intelligence, like John Conway, to design the rules of the game. It did not happen just by chance. Similarly, in the case of the universe, for a mind to think of the values of human life, and then design a Big Bang in order to realise those values, would require vast intelligence and originating power. Almost everyone agrees that our universe looks designed in this sense. Yet many biologists do not believe in God. Why is this?

It is partly because they think of God in a naive way, as a person who is always interfering in the world from outside. Partly it is because the evolutionary process can look wasteful and violent. And partly it is because there seems to be quite a lot of chance in the process. I have suggested that you should not begin by thinking of something like an invisible human-like person just outside (or 'above') the universe. You should think, instead, of a vast cosmic intelligence aiming at values which must be self-organising to a large extent, and which must be realised in an open and emergent universe. This intelligence gives the universe a direction and goal, and decrees that the universe will operate in accordance with general intelligible laws, to allow for regularity and, later in the process, for predictability and control by intelligences generated within the universe. Many features are, however, left undetermined, to allow for creativity and novelty and, later in the process, for conscious freedom.

Many people who are sympathetic to the idea of purpose in the universe look for an alternative to God, even though a creative intelligence seems the most adequate explanation of how things are. I shall just mention two. One is the many-worlds hypothesis. This universe, with its seemingly purposive structure, may seem especially improbable, on grounds of chance alone. But if there are zillions of universes, each of which has to exist, then sooner or later this one will exist. The improbability will have disappeared.

In fact, however, the improbability will have increased immensely. What ensures that every one of those universes will actually exist? If the existence of one universe is improbable, the existence of zillions of them seems to be zillions of times more improbable. Well, goes the reply, the point is that there is only one super-reality, the quantum vacuum, with one set of quantum laws, and it gives rise to all those universes. But how improbable is that? I doubt if anyone can assess such a probability at all. In which case the many-worlds theory is not more probable than the God theory after all.

You just have to make a choice between more or less equally probable or improbable things. Either zillions of universes (which we can never observe or confirm) or one cosmic intelligence. Either way you have this apparently purposive universe, which ends up with values of consciousness and reason that are not even parts of the many-worlds theory. If those values are real and irreducible to matter, God, in whose mind such values really exist, seems to be the better explanation.

The other interesting alternative to God is Thomas Nagel's theory that the universe is purposive, but that purpose is internal to the universe itself. It is not 'imposed' from outside by a God. Rather, we are to think of the basic entities of the universe as pan-psychic – that it, every entity has both a material 'outside' and a mental 'inside'. The two sides necessarily go together, and together they develop from simple particles, where presumably the mental side is minimal, to complex brains, where the mental side exhibits self-consciousness and reason. At that late state, the mental side actually plays an active role, since we humans act in accordance with reasons, so some causality comes most of all from the mental side, even though the two sides remain stuck together.

Nagel agrees that the purposive development is towards greater value, and that the whole process exists for the sake of realising values. This is an intriguing theory, but it is very hard to see in what sense the goal of fully rational action could be inherent in the very simple first states of the undeveloped universe. Nagel's idea is that there would just be an innate probabilistic tendency towards rationality and value. Even Aristotle, who had a similar theory, had to postulate a perfect trans-temporal God who could actually envisage the goal and attract physical entities towards it.[16] It looks as if the goal cannot be within the universe itself, but must be in a mind which is already developed and fully actual.

Perhaps it would help if we said that the mind of God is not completely separate from the physical universe. Maybe it expresses itself in the universe, so that the universe is a physical manifestation of Spirit, and Spirit both contains and constrains the physical universe, while leaving it creatively free to develop in its own way to a large extent. Perhaps the mind of God is the mind of the universe itself, and that mind participates and is expressed in all the vicissitudes and creative experiments of cosmic history. The medieval Indian philosopher Ramanuja called the universe 'the body of the Lord', and maybe that is a metaphor which has renewed relevance in today's scientific world-picture.[17]

Such a hypothesis seems to meet Nagel's main objections to God, and to be at least as coherent as his theory – perhaps more coherent, because the idea of a goal just floating around on its own does not seem plausible. Purposes, as we understand them normally, have to be imagined by minds. So putting the idea of a purpose for the universe in the mind of God gives it a sort of reality we can at least roughly understand. And of course if God is the creator of the universe, you can see how that idea could have causal influence, and affect the way the ordinary causal laws of the universe work out.

So I think that the complexity, integration and apparent purposiveness of the universe as it is observed by modern science is good evidence for God, or for Spirit. As Fred Hoyle wrote, 'I do not believe that any scientist who examined the evidence would fail to draw the inference that the laws of nuclear physics have been deliberately designed with regard to the consequences they produce inside the stars'[18] – and, I would add, that they produce in the emergence of intelligent life. We should not let the derision of materialists undermine this thought, which flowed from the pen of a noted atheist. It shows the strength of the evidence for Spirit, when you have not been brow-beaten by the rhetoric of materialism.

The idealist point of view

To sum up the points I have made in the last three chapters, I have argued that it is important evidence for Spirit that idealism is a major and widely held philosophical world view. Idealists usually hold that a cosmic mind or Spirit is the reality underlying the physical cosmos, and that it drives the cosmos towards a goal or goals of intrinsic value. I have considered some philosophical arguments that would support the belief that there is discernible purpose in the cosmos, and that the existence of suffering and evil is compatible with the existence of such purpose. These arguments, at least in the European tradition, are usually framed in terms of

God as a supremely valuable creator of the universe. But idealists do not always use the concept of God, and the arguments could also be phrased by talking, as some of them do, about 'the Absolute' or Spirit.

There are a number of versions of Idealism, but the philosophical view which opposes them all is materialism. Materialism is a very controversial theory, and it is important to remember that it is a philosophical theory – it is not a scientifically established fact, by any means. For most people, it is obvious that perceptions, images, sensations, thoughts, and feelings, all exist and cannot simply be identified with material states of the brain or of anything else. Among philosophical theories, that basically leaves dualism – mind and matter are different sorts of things; monism – there is only one thing, which has both mental and physical aspects; and idealism – mind is the basic reality, on which matter depends.

If you ask what sort of evidence there is for these theories, it is obvious that there are no facts of experience that some people have and others lack. The evidence will not consist of new facts. It will be a matter of interpreting the facts in the most elegant, consistent, coherent, comprehensive, and fruitful way. That in turn will be a matter of judgment, and different philosophers will, and do, disagree. You will point to bits of experience that seem to support your interpretation and lower the plausibility of other interpretations. But none of them will be decisive.

Stephen Hawking thinks that this sort of philosophising is dead, and has been replaced by science (*The Grand Design*, p. 13). But he is simply assuming that materialism is true (in one very sophisticated version), so that the question of interpretation is solved. But it is not solved, and there is no universally accepted way, even among the most competent judges, of agreeing on a solution.

This might be annoying, but all honest philosophers know that it is true. Thomas Nagel says, 'In every area of thought we must rely ultimately on our judgments, tested by reflection, subject to correction by the counter-arguments of others, modified by the imagination and by comparison with alternatives' (*Mind and*

Cosmos, p. 103). Nagel originated the haunting expression, 'A view from nowhere', and argued forcefully that no one has a view from nowhere. We all start somewhere, with a particular place in history and geography, and a particular perspective that we have been taught or picked up in our early lives. So believing in God, for example, is not something all of us have to argue for, starting from some neutral ground where we do not yet believe anything.

Some of us start from belief that mind is the basis of all things, and matter is its manifestation. Some of us start with no such belief, but perhaps with a predisposition to think that the things we see and touch are real, and everything else is just an abstraction. Others of us are born materialists, and we fall in love with reductionist science, and hardly pay any attention to spiritual things. We have differing fundamental perspectives, and the best philosophers can think of no way to gain agreement between all intelligent and informed people. All we can then do is confront alternative views to our own, see if they have anything to say to us, and try to make our initial view as coherent with our growing knowledge as we can. We may need to give up our initial view, but usually it is not as bad as that, and we just have to adjust it. How far we can adjust a view without giving it up is a matter of personal judgment, and of whether other people take to our adjustments or reject them out of hand.

I am by nature an idealist. I was an idealist before I had ever heard of idealism. I always thought that the world of ordinary everyday beliefs and sense-experiences was only an appearance of something deeper. I suppose I had a sense of the transitory nature of things, of their essential lack of substantial being, of their dependence on frail human faculties of perception and thought. We see sights, hear sounds, feel touches, and out of them we construct a picture of a world of solid enduring objects. But the only world we immediately know is the world of our perceptions.

What lies beneath our perceptions is unseen and unsensed, except in the intimations of transcendence that come to us in music and art, or in the demands of morality, in speculations about the new and strange reality of the quantum world, and in feelings that in our commerce with other persons we occasionally reach out into depths beyond appearance and social convention.

In all these ways I never felt myself going beyond the everyday into an encounter with something alien and intractable, something like the mechanical world of classical physics, without value or purpose or intrinsic significance, so that humans stand heroically and self-consciously alone facing the bleakness of a pitiless universe. On the contrary, I felt that the scientific picture of an unconscious blind and accidental universe was itself an abstraction even from the world of sensory appearance. What I encountered beyond the everyday was not unconscious and alien. It was beautiful (disclosed in moments of transcendent beauty), good (disclosed in moments of moral demand and inspiration), true (disclosed in revelations of the mathematical elegance and complexity and integration of nature), and mind-like (disclosed in experiences of genuine love).

At these points, I felt, I touched what was most truly real. And since reality is one and indivisible, I touched or apprehended the one unseen Spirit that, in Dante's words, 'moves the sun and other stars', and is the substantial ground that underlies the abstractions of natural science and the appearances of the sensory world alike. That, I think, is what really moves me, the perspective which defines what I see and how I see things.

I am not an idealist because I can prove, starting from nowhere, that matter cannot exist without mind. I am an idealist because what I feel most deeply is that human experience, justly discerned, is the medium of values and ideals that could not exist without something mind-like at the root of things. And from that root springs all the rich diversity of the world in which we think and feel and live. That is the Idealist world-picture, and it can be the foundation of a profound human spirituality.

7.

―――――∞――――――

SPIRITUAL VALUES IN SCIENCE

The elimination of mind

Idealism is a philosophical view, one that attempts to think about the ultimate nature of reality. It is not science, though it needs to take account of the findings of science if it is to have any hope of being plausible. But scientists themselves, especially in physics and more especially in quantum physics and cosmology, sometimes adventure into philosophical questions about what is ultimately real. I now want to suggest that in the quest for scientific understanding of nature, there are also signs of transcendence, of realities deeper and more mysterious than things that seem obvious to our senses. In 2010 Stephen Hawking wrote a book – *The Grand Design* – that is of great interest for what it says about such matters, and I will take that book as a starting-point for what I have to say.

In this book, Stephen Hawking agrees that we should attempt to answer the questions 'Why is there something rather than nothing? Why do we exist?' and 'Why this particular set of laws and not some other?' (p. 19). In his book he proposes to answer those questions, from a purely scientific point of view ('Philosophy is dead', he announces on p. 13, even though the whole book is an exercise in scientifically informed philosophy). But there is something very odd about this. Nowhere in the book does he mention consciousness, value, or thought. In fact he finally gives the game away on p. 228 by saying, 'we human beings ... are ourselves mere collections of fundamental particles'. That is a philosophical view if ever there was one! It is precisely what is usually called eliminative materialism. It reduces consciousness, feelings and thoughts to nothing but complicated arrangements of physical particles, and thereby eliminates them from reality. I regard this as a non-starter, if you want to give a complete explanation of the universe.

Science is a set of theoretical postulates to explain and predict observations. It therefore should not ever be used to say that those observations do not exist – reductionism is not a theory in science. Reductionism is a sophisticated but, in my view, desperate philosophical attempt to deny that there are any minds to which physical things appear. It is an attempt to deny that consciousness, mind, purpose, and value have any ultimately real existence. But since all our theories are based on conscious experiences, this attempt seems to be self-defeating from the start.

The world of physics is a world without consciousness, value, and purpose. Those terms simply do not occur in physics. What this suggests is that physics misses out some very important features of reality. It speaks only of the physical features of things, but does not speak of consciousness and its contents. I think the obvious conclusion is that physics tells us some very important things about the world, and explains how our observations occur as they do. But it does not explain the fact that we have minds which are conscious of observations in the first place – even though we would know nothing about physics if we had no minds.

If you seriously want to tackle the question 'Why do we exist?', you have to begin by accepting that we are conscious, thinking, feeling beings, and not 'mere collections of particles'. No purely physical account of the universe can explain consciousness, thought, and feeling. Let me modify that blunt statement a little. If you are a reductionist, then consciousness can be explained in purely physical terms. But no one has come anywhere near providing a comprehensive and convincing account of reductionism. Even hard-line materialists usually admit that the problem of explaining consciousness is the 'hard problem' in science, and that we are nowhere near solving it. And if philosophy is not quite dead, maybe many half-alive philosophers would say that it is not just a hard but an insoluble problem if you are trying to do it in purely physical terms. Because thoughts and feelings are just not physical.

At this point we all have to agree that there are some basic philosophical questions that do not look as if they are ever going to have agreed answers. The problem of mind and body is one of them, perhaps the most basic one of all. For people like me, the evidence that thoughts and feelings are real is indisputable, obvious, and completely convincing. It consists of my thoughts and feelings, which nobody else knows, or can know, in the way that I do. But for many people the findings of physical science are so compelling that they simply cannot admit that there could be anything it does not explain, at least in principle. And there you are! Stalemate!

Fundamental perspectives

In this situation, the only reasonable thing to do is to admit that the evidence is not universally compelling, in that it will never be agreed. Yet it can seem completely convincing to people who disagree completely about what the evidence implies. Questions about such evidence are inherently unsettlable. To one group of people (apparently including Stephen Hawking) a completely convincing explanation of why we exist can be given in purely physical terms about how the universe originated from a quantum vacuum in accordance with the laws of a very complicated theory called M-theory (which has not been worked out yet). But to another group of people (including Thomas Nagel and me) any complete explanation of why we exist must somehow include and unite both physical factors of cosmic evolution and some explanation of how mind and consciousness are central to the existence of the universe. Philosophers have argued with each other and scientists have argued with each other interminably about this, and we know we are not all going to agree. That does not stop us thinking that our views are wholly reasonable. What we get out of this discussion are two main points: there are unsettlable questions, and good evidence does not have to be universally compelling.[19]

The quantum vacuum

Although Hawking ignores questions about mind and value, he does offer an explanation of the universe in terms of a non-physical reality with the properties of eternity and necessity. This is because he explains the origin of the universe, at the 'Big Bang', by saying that it arises from the quantum vacuum and from quantum laws. Now whatever the quantum vacuum is, it is beyond the time of our universe. That is, it is eternal. And quantum laws, being elegant mathematical laws, are in some sense necessary. That is because mathematics cannot be any other than it is. Mathematical truths do not just happen to be true; they have to be true; there is no alternative.

You may say that there could be different axioms in mathematics, and that is the case. But the whole set of mathematical truths, including all the axioms there could possibly be, is necessarily what it is. And it could be that there is only one set of mathematical truths (of quantum laws) that could give rise to a universe containing carbon-based intelligent life-forms like us.

In fact, Hawking proposes that all mathematically possible combinations actually give rise to actual universes. Perhaps, he says, for technical reasons there could be 10 to the power of 500 universes – that is an enormous number of universes. But the vast majority of them would never give rise to the conditions that make intelligent life possible. Maybe only a few, maybe only one, possible universes can give rise to life-forms like us.

On this theory, many forms of necessity are involved. There is the necessity of the whole array of possible mathematical systems. There is the necessity that these systems give rise to actual universes. There is the necessity that, once universes exist, they will obey just one set of mathematical laws exactly and without fail. And there is the necessity that one of these universes (ours) will eventually give rise to intelligent life.

If all this was true, it would indeed explain the nature of our universe very satisfactorily. By the necessary laws of mathematics, which are eternally true, every mathematically possible universe will exist, and at least one of them would necessarily give rise to us. We are no longer a surprising accident. We are completely explained!

We, and the whole universe, are dependent upon a time-transcending (eternal) and necessary (mathematically modelled) reality (the quantum vacuum plus the quantum laws), and we necessarily arise from it, just as we are. This theory is uncannily like the theory of God, an eternal and necessary reality from which the universe arises. Yet it is proposed as a competitor with God, whom, Hawking says, we no longer need. But is it really a competitor, or is it maybe just a partial and truncated view of God?

8.

EXPLAINING THE UNIVERSE

Absolute explanations

Anybody who thinks minds, with their thoughts and feelings, values and purposes, need to be explained, as well as physical particles, will find something deficient about the Hawking hypothesis. Because the fact is that, far from explaining minds, he never once mentions them. It is as though they did not exist – even though his theory only exists because it was invented by a very rational mind, and almost entirely by pure thought.

It is obvious that the Hawking hypothesis is very speculative, and highly disputed among mathematical physicists. But nobody says it is stupid, or superstitious, or that there is no evidence for it. Hawking sets out his criteria for a good explanation on page 68 of his book. A good explanation has to be elegant, contain few arbitrary elements, agree with all existing observations, and make detailed predictions about the future. M-theory, he says, is elegant, and it is consistent with the best scientific knowledge. Does it contain few arbitrary elements? Well, you might think that postulating 10 (500) universe is a bit arbitrary. On the other hand, it follows from a very elegant theory, and that is not arbitrary, even if it seems rather excessive. Does it make detailed predictions about the future? Not directly, because it is far from complete as yet. But it is a key part of a whole system more specific parts of which do make such predictions, and they have all been confirmed to a great degree of accuracy.

Could you say this about the theory of God, a 'mind of the universe', too? It is elegant, because it posits just one ultimate being from which the whole complete universe originates, and it provides just one ultimate principle for originating a universe – for the sake of the distinctive values that the universe makes possible. It is, or in many versions it is, compatible with all existing observations. It contains no arbitrary assumptions – unless God is thought to be an arbitrary assumption. But if the existence of human minds needs explaining, it seems that in some sense mind will have to be seen as a basic and irreducible constituent of the universe, and God certainly fulfils that role.

The God theory is not a scientific theory because it makes no detailed predictions about the future. That is hardly surprising, since the God theory is not meant to be a scientific theory. It does make some predictions – goodness will triumph, evil will be eliminated, the righteous will see God. But these predictions are not testable at the moment, and mostly lie far in the future, or even in some other form of existence. The job of the God theory is not, however, to provide predictions. It is to provide a basis for believing that the universe, and each life in particular, has a unique and valuable purpose which is given to it by a being of supreme perfection and power who can ensure that purpose will be realised.

Scientific theories are practically useful because they enable us to predict and so to use physical features of the world for our well-being. The theory of God is practically useful because it enables us to see what true human well-being is (what the true human purpose is), and how to achieve it. Even when we say something as abstract sounding as: 'God is eternal and necessary', we are in fact saying something of immense practical usefulness. We are saying that the being who gives value to human life and promises its realisation cannot be weakened or destroyed by time (is eternal) and will never change in love, compassion, and care for us and for all sentient beings (is necessary). Even the most abstract thoughts about God have a real and immediate practical importance, and those abstract thoughts are the results of pursuing the grounds for our trust and confidence in God as far as we can.

The belief that God is eternal and necessary is based on the development of an elegant explanatory theory for explaining why the universe is the way it is, and why we exist. Such explanations, according to Hawking and to many others, would ideally end in a reality that was eternal and necessary. That is because natural science works by pursuing the question, 'Why did this happen?' as far as it possibly can. Physicists used to think that you could not get beyond the Big Bang, and you just had to accept that as a brute inexplicable fact. But with the rise of quantum physics, cosmologists have pressed their questions further, and now try to explain the origin of space and time by showing that it arises from the quantum vacuum by necessity.

Once you get to a timeless reality, you can no longer ask 'What caused this to happen?' because no other being could cause an eternal being to exist (could bring it into existence). Once you get to a necessary reality, you can no longer ask, 'Why did this happen?' because there is no alternative to it. We cannot know for certain that there is an eternal and necessary reality, but as a postulate it finally answers all scientific questions about why the universe exists by saying it has its origin in a reality that could not be otherwise and logically could have no cause. That would be the final and absolute explanation of the universe, and it would be very satisfying for a physicist.

A philosopher cannot fail to notice that this is a replay of the first three of Thomas Aquinas' 'Five Ways of demonstrating the existence of God'. The universe must have an uncaused, changeless, and necessary cause if we are to have an absolute explanation of its existence. As every student of Aquinas' arguments knows, there does not *have* to be an absolute explanation of the universe. Perhaps the very idea of a necessary being is incoherent. Maybe it is not even true that every event has to have a cause, or that there is a reason for everything.

It is generally agreed that these arguments are not demonstrative proofs, which will convince any reasonable person. To find them convincing, you have to accept that the universe is intelligible (there is a reason for everything), that the idea of necessary existence makes sense, and that there is an absolute explanation for the universe (the universe is not just an accident or an inexplicable brute fact). There is no proof of these beliefs. But many notable scientists (including Stephen Hawking) do seem to accept them. They are very reasonable beliefs to have. Maybe they are implicit in the practice of science and are basic assumptions that are conditions of finding the universe fully rational.

Is there evidence for these beliefs? It seems that the great success of the sciences is evidence for the intelligibility of the universe, and that the similar success of pure mathematics is evidence for the coherence of necessary truths. The main evidence lies in the elegance, consistency, coherence, and explanatory power of the postulate of an eternal and necessary being. That makes it rationally acceptable, though it cannot compel assent, and there will always be disagreements about it. Like some other evidence for God, it is strong but essentially disputable. As I have suggested, there is nothing wrong with that, from a rational point of view.

The principle of axiology

Despite the similarity of Hawking's theory to the arguments of Aquinas (which themselves derive from Aristotle), Hawking offers his theory as an alternative to God, not as part of a 'proof' of God. I think this is mostly due to his complete neglect of mind, value, consciousness, and purpose in the universe. If mind is an irreducible element of reality, which cannot be completely explained in purely physical terms, mind will have to enter into any absolute explanation of the universe in some way. All Hawking offers is mathematically beautiful laws and various complex forms of energy in their lowest energy states (the quantum vacuum), which exist and act by blind necessity.

If you add mind to this mix, you have something which is conscious of those laws and operates on a principle that is not part of natural science. That is the *principle of axiology*, by which I mean: bringing something about for the sake of some future value. Minds, as we know them, typically operate by thinking of possible future states which they prefer or value, and then acting so as to make those states actually exist. Minds, in other words, act to make possible states into actual states, to realise potentialities for the sake of obtaining actual states that they value.

Thinking of possible states is, as far as we know, something that only quite sophisticated minds do. It involves being in an actual state (a state of thinking about the future) which internally refers to a possible state, to something beyond itself. The mental state is not just an actual state; it is *about* something that does not exist. This 'aboutness' is a property that only minds have – philosophers call it 'intentionality'. It shows that thoughts about the future cannot be reduced to a physical description of minds in the present.

The other main property that only minds have is the ability to act in order to make such thoughts into actual things. I think about the nice taste of ice cream, and go out to buy one, in order to enjoy the state I have just thought of. Minds have intentional thoughts, and act in intentional ways. That, in short, is the distinctively mental principle of conscious purpose or axiology.

This suggests that if mind must enter into the absolute explanation of the universe, there must be some place for purpose and value among the ultimate principles of the universe.

This is actually helpful in solving the problem of how purely mathematical laws can govern the ultimate energies of the universe, and of how we can be sure that they will continue to do so. That is a real problem for Hawking. As he famously asked, 'What is it that breathes fire into equations?' That is, what gives mere mathematical equations, passive and inert as they seem to be, the power to give rise to actual physical universes, and continue to run them in predictable ways?

If there is a mind which is aware of all those equations, which knows how they would govern physical states if they were applied to physical energies, then that mind could choose to make some of those laws apply to basic energies for the sake of outcomes which the mind values. The principle of axiology could apply to the universe. We would not then have to say that all possible universes arise by blind necessity. We would say that the mind that conceives all possible universes chooses to create one or more of them for the sake of producing states which it values.

The mind of God

If you wanted to appeal to Occam's Razor – that you should choose the theory that appeals to the fewest number of entities – you would unhesitatingly choose such an originating mind over the necessary existing of 10 (+500 zeros) universes. Necessity would no longer be blind. Given a primordial cosmic mind, it would originate a universe for a good reason – and it would not originate zillions of spare universes for which there was no good reason. The principle of axiology, which only minds can operate, provides an elegant selection-principle for originating specific universes. The universe will not just emanate unconsciously for the primordial vacuum. It will be created by rational choice from the primordial ocean of possibilities which are a necessary part of the mind of God.

This seems such a good theory that it seems odd that Hawking does not take it more seriously. I think there are various reasons for this, but I do not think any of them are very strong. One is the reductionist theory that minds are nothing but collections of physical particles, so a cosmic mind that was not physical could not exist. This view collapses if you think that thoughts, feelings, and perceptions are different in kind from physical particles. Even if you think that human minds do not exist without physical brains, this seems to be a matter of fact, not a necessary truth. In other words, a being could have thoughts and feelings even if it had no brain. We are not likely to find this out by any physical experiment. But a simple thought-experiment – just imagine having a view of Mount Everest without having a body, a brain, or eyes to see with – seems to demonstrate that, though we do not think it is going to happen to us, it is perfectly possible.

I do not think it is at all difficult to think of a cosmic mind that knows many things about the universe, and can do many things in the universe, but has no brain or body. Of course that does not show there is such a mind. It shows that, as far as we can see, there could be a non-human mind that was not a collection of physical particles. If we can postulate eternal and necessary laws and energies as the basis of the universe, we can equally easily postulate an eternal and necessary mind, as an elegant theory to explain why the universe exists.

But Hawking says that God is not needed. A scientific explanation is enough – 'the beginning of the universe was governed by the laws of science and doesn't need to be set in motion by some god' (p. 173). This is basically an argument that we should go for the simplest explanation. But it seems simpler to have one cosmic mind than to have a whole battery of separate mathematical laws and forces and fields like gravity, inflation, electric charge, spin, and so on, which have no very obvious connection with one another. If they were all elements of one mind, that would give unity and integration to such laws and energies, which would be a great gain in simplicity. The God theory would also eliminate vast numbers of spare universes, and leave just a few very interesting, complex, and valuable universes, which is another gain in simplicity.

In any case, simplicity should not be bought at the price of ignoring consciousness and value. A simple theory should also be comprehensive, so any satisfactory theory of everything must include minds as well as physical states in some way. There are a number of theories that might do this, but mind-like explanations have an explanatory advantage over physical theories. Whereas a purely physical theory cannot account for consciousness, a theory of cosmic intelligence is able to account for matter in a very satisfactory way. A material universe provides the environment for generating consciousness, gives objects of knowledge for consciousness, and provides a theatre of operations in which many minds can act and co-operate in action. A world of many finite minds needs some sort of physical universe, whereas a physical universe does not need, and cannot really account for, the existence of minds. So a mind theory of the universe is more inclusive and comprehensive than a purely materialistic theory. That has to be a good thing.

A key statement in Hawking's account is that God is not needed to 'set the universe in motion'. It is as though the physical account of the universe is complete, except for one thing, its starting point. If you can eliminate the need for a starting point, you eliminate the need for God. For some physicists, God only had that one job left anyway, having been made redundant from all God's traditional jobs, so not much is lost if you dispense with God altogether.

That is not, however, the point. Nobody seriously thinks that God just sets the universe going, and then ignores it altogether. The real question is not whether somebody had to push-start the universe, but whether the whole universe, at every moment, depends on some deeper reality beyond itself. Hawking obviously thinks it does, because on his theory the whole observable universe depends upon the quantum laws which exist apart from any particular universe, and the vacuum energies whose continued operation keep every universe going. Without those laws and energies, the observable universe would collapse. The universe does not keep going by itself. It is a consequence (almost a by-product) of deeper goings on beyond our space-time.

The theist agrees absolutely that this space-time is not capable of keeping going by itself. It depends upon some deeper reality which is beyond space and time and is necessary and self-sustaining in some profound sense. The theist agrees that the deeper reality is intelligible (not just accidental or arbitrary), conceptually elegant and beautiful, and the ultimate source of awe-inspiring powers and energies. All the theist adds to this is that the deeper reality is conscious and purposive, not blind and pointless. This cosmic mind does not just set the universe going. Without its continued existence and support, the universe would not exist at all.

The deepest reality is mind, eternal and necessary mind. Without that mind, the laws of science would not be recognised and applied to any universe, and they would not lead to the existence of conscious intelligent agents, to a universe which understands its own nature. Mind really is essential to the existence of a universe like ours, and probably to the existence of any universe at all.

9.

⸻

SCIENCE AND MIND

How minds create reality

Strange as it may seem, there are strong hints of such a view in
Hawking's theory. I have said that he did not mention mind and
consciousness at all. But that is not quite right. He spends some
time explaining the two-slit experiment in quantum theory. The
results of this experiment can be put rather crudely by saying that
particles like photons behave like waves when they are not being
measured or observed, but they behave like particles when they are
being measured. This very odd result was said by Richard Feynman
to contain all the mysteries of quantum mechanics. In the two-slit
experiment, sub-atomic particles are shot at a wall with two slits in
it, and then hit a detection screen. If one slit is closed, what you see
is the impact of a particle. It seems that the particle has just gone
through one slit. But if both slits are open, you see the impact of a
wave. It seems that the particle has gone through both slits.

It is hard to say why this is so. But things get worse. If you keep
both slits open, but observe one slit, so that you know which slit
a particle goes through, the particle will behave just like a particle.
But if you do not observe the slits, it will behave like a wave. It
seems that the fact of observing which slit a particle goes through
changes the object from a wave to a particle. Observation changes
what is observed.

This is bad enough. But things are even worse. In what is called
the 'delayed-choice experiment', Feynman delayed observing a
particle until *after* it has passed through the two slits and just *before*

it hits the detection screen. Again, the observation collapses a wave into a particle. But now it does so after the particle has 'decided' to go through either one or both slits. It looks as though, as Hawking puts it, 'observations you make on a system in the present affect its past' (p. 106). Our present observation seems to cause the particle to go through one slit instead of two – but that had already happened before we made the observation.

This is seriously weird. What Hawking proposes is that 'the universe doesn't have just a single history, but every possible history … and our observations in its current state affect its past and determine the different histories of the universe' (p. 107). In other words, everything that is possible happens, but observations can make it the case that just one thing has happened, after all, at least as far as we are concerned, or in the universe-slice in which we exist.

He concludes with the astonishing claim that 'we create history by our observation, rather than history creating us' (p. 179). So 'the universe does not have a unique observer-independent history'. It is very hard to know what to make of all this. But one way of thinking about it is to say that observations collapse wave-functions, which speak of many possible universes, into particles, which are states of an actual universe. In other words, it is minds (the things which make observations, after all) that make physical things, the things we observe, actual.

If so, Hawking does give an important place to observing minds. Minds make possibilities actual. They 'create history'. And if the universe is not observer-independent, then there must be some observer to make the universe actual. I think it is obvious that the observer is not any human being. We come late in the history of the universe, and it really is pushing things a bit far to say that the Big Bang was not actual until some human being 'observed' it – and, of course, no human being has actually observed the Big Bang at all. It seems to call for an observer who existed even at the beginning of the universe. And that really is very like God.

If some mind is needed to make possibilities actual, it is even more plausible to think that possibilities cannot just exist on their own. If they exist at all, they must exist in something actual. That cannot be just the set of possibilities itself, since a whole lot of possibilities is still no more than possible. A good candidate is the same cosmic mind as the one that makes some possibilities actual – namely, God.

All this no doubt seems very abstract and very weird. But at least we can see that the God theory is no more weird than some interpretations of quantum mechanics. It has a lot to be said for it, as an elegant and comprehensive theory. And there is good evidence for it, both in the demand for a 'Theory of Everything', and in some of the more mind-stretching experiments of quantum mechanics.

Most people do not believe in God because God is a good absolute explanation of the universe. That is not their main reason for believing. The main reason is likely to lie in experiences of a certain sort. But the question will always remain of what the most adequate description of the object of such experiences is. At that point questions of moral adequacy (universality and personal fulfilment) and explanatory force (coherence, integration, comprehensiveness, and elegance) arise.

At that point it is important that God is up there with the best scientific theories as an absolute explanation for the universe. Hawking's theory is much nearer to God than he thinks. So I think that idealism should be taken seriously, not as a competitor with, but as a supplement and adjustment to Hawking's theory which reinforces the claim that mind is the basis and best explanation of the physical universe.

Theistic idealism

There is a view of evidence for a spiritual reality like God that goes like this: we live in a world of physical objects, among which are other human beings. We have evidence that these human beings have minds, because they act in purposive ways, display emotional reactions, and speak to us. If there was a God, a cosmic mind, evidence would have to be some sort of behaviour or speech that put that beyond doubt. It might be writing in the sky: 'I am God. Take care'. Or it might be some sort of behaviour by rocks, trees and clouds that seemed to respond to our prayers or wishes, like rain coming whenever we ask for it, or earthquakes occurring when we do wrong, and stopping when we repent. But these things do not happen. So there is no evidence for God.

This is a completely misguided approach. It misconstrues the sort of evidence that is in question. The basic question is whether our world of physical objects is good evidence for what reality is like. Or is there evidence that the world that appears to us is largely a construct of the mind, and there is an underlying, largely hidden, reality with a deeper intelligibility, value, and purpose?

Such evidence will not be evidence of another physical or finite object. It will have to be evidence that puts the whole finite world of experience in question, evidence for a deeper reality. We may not know what this reality is like in its inner nature, since it will be inaccessible to direct observation and probably beyond the full comprehension of human minds. But it will have to be such as to give rise both to the intelligible and morally neutral operation of the laws of the physical universe and to the consciousness, value, reason, and intentionality that we see in human lives.

The former, physical, aspect of things is amenable to a reductionist analysis, so that you can think of it as a product of a few simple laws and a few basic forces – something like the M-theory postulate of Stephen Hawking. Even then, however, there are puzzles about the elegance and intelligibility of these laws, their astonishing ability to obey complex mathematical patterns, and their seemingly inevitable tendency to form integrated complex systems, which suggest something more than a purely accidental or random existence.

The conscious, reasoning, valuing, aspect of things, however, seems to require a purposive ordering towards value in the fundamental structure of reality. For as both Aristotle and Thomas Aquinas said, things are moved towards an end by intelligence, by a mind which can envisage a goal of value, and move things towards that goal.

It is not just the fact of experience, but reflection on the nature of experience, that can lead to the postulation of such a reality, an eternal and necessary mind of supreme value which is the ultimate source and basis of our experienced world.

10.

SPIRITUAL VALUES IN RELIGION

The gods of ancient religion

One major area of human life that is not so important in a heavily secularised Europe, but is still of fundamental importance throughout the world as a whole, is religion. The rituals of religion, the varied forms of religious life, and the systems of symbols and metaphors which frame the doctrines and stories of religion, have great meaning for millions of human beings. I can be deeply moved by choral music in great Christian cathedrals. And presumably it is not just the music. Something about the place, the atmosphere, and the ambience, contribute to a distinctive sense of transcendent meaning and significance.

Perhaps we should not attempt to translate these ritual events into prosaic sentences – maybe that is what is wrong with much theology. But one result of the secularisation of society is that the whole meaning of religious ceremonies is in danger of being lost, because people have simply forgotten how to interpret it. Not everyone likes the practices of religion, but those who do cultivate a certain sort of sensibility to what can be called generally idealist views – views which give priority to the spiritual realities which can be conveyed through physical sounds, smells, and sights. If that sensibility is translated into scientific language, it gets totally lost, and religion is totally misinterpreted.

Materialist philosophers tend to have no sympathy with idealist or religious views, or with talk of objective values and ideals. This leads them to an inability to understand religious beliefs, or even what the character of such beliefs is. When materialists talk about religion, religious believers often simply cannot recognise what they are talking about.

A good example of this is the attempt of some materialists to give an account of early (often called 'primitive') religions. They feel on very safe ground here, for doesn't everyone know that the ancient religions were all false? So we don't have to bother about truth. When materialists talk about early religion, about the gods of ancient Greece, for example, they tend to regard those gods as primitive scientific attempts to explain why things happen. Zeus is seen as a primitive explanation of why thunderstorms happen – a supernatural being makes them happen for some unknown reason. It is not surprising that the ancient gods faded away. They were just bad scientific explanations.

But such crude interpretations seem to be badly mistaken. The ancient gods, and the spirits of nature, are not scientific explanations at all. They are more like what I have called axiological explanations. They are concerned with pointing to things of value, that are worth aiming at just for their own sakes. They are poetic ways of speaking of the awesome and beautiful powers of the natural and moral worlds. They express the depths of significance that are conveyed in and through the powers of nature, and the moral demands and complexities that mark human lives. But they are not literalistic beliefs that there are immortal beings living on Mount Olympus. (Olympus is quite a low mountain, and one easily climbable to look for any literal gods).

These ancient stories had not yet been rationalised and moralised. That is, the powers, virtues, and ideals that the gods symbolise had not yet been integrated into a simple, elegant, unitary, coherent, and comprehensive scheme of interpretation. The taboos and customs of ancient tribal societies had not yet been integrated into a more universal moral system of general principles.

This process of integration happened in Indian religious history as all the local gods came to be seen as aspects of one supreme spiritual reality – *Brahman*. It happened in Middle Eastern religious history as all the local gods were supplanted by one simple and unitary reality with a universal and rational moral purpose – the local God of Abraham and Isaac became the universal and only God of Isaiah and the prophets. Such a process of integration did happen in the major religious traditions of the world. But it is important to see that what were being integrated were not incorrect scientific theories. They were intuitions of transcendence, of spiritual dimensions of reality that were felt to be experienced and apprehended in and through significant personal and historical events. If you miss that element, you miss the heart of religion and the roots of developed belief in God.

Forms of spirituality and religion

There is a widespread feeling in many Western societies that there is a place for spirituality – for a counterblast to materialism, which flattens out everything of value in human life into a set of accidental collisions of sub-atomic particles, and can promote a way of life centred on the importance of material, egoistic, short-term values. But there is also a widespread feeling that religion has become not only obsolete, but that it is actually an obstacle to moral and intellectual progress. The moral codes of much religion, founded for the most part on the ancient taboos and prejudices of ancient Patriarchal societies, stand in the way of free rational thinking about the best way to live. And commitment to literal versions of various creation myths and a general short-sightedness about the vast extent of space and time brings much religion into conflict with modern science. Add to that all the hypocrisies of religious preachers, and all the violence caused by misguided zealots who think they have to exterminate everyone who disagrees with them, and it is not surprising that religion has a bad press in all reasonably enlightened societies.

While all that is true, we would be losing much of enormous value in human life if we entirely ignored the teachings of the great religious teachers in human history. The Buddha, Sankara, Ramanuja, Jesus, Mohammed, Baha'U'llah, Guru Nanak, and many others have taught ways of overcoming hatred, greed and egoism, and of becoming aware of a deeper spiritual reality, an awareness of the value, beauty and purpose of being that can transform the quality of human life for the better.

There are thousands of religions in the world, and of course they do not all say the same thing. Disciples who have formalised the teachings of their spiritual masters have tended to erect dogmatic and exclusive systems, and turn paths of spiritual practice and enlightenment into rigid creeds to be accepted on authority. They have not always done so, and the original vision of the major religious teachers often remains, perhaps in the less visible and powerful parts of religious systems. But if we see the spiritual realm as existing in and expressed through the physical realm, it will seem natural that the very different physical environments, geographical conditions, and historical developments within human cultures, will give rise to different perspectives on spiritual reality.

Three main streams of religious thinking and practice are usually picked out by historians of religion as important.[20] In what is sometimes called the Abrahamic stream, originating in the Middle East, awareness of Spirit gets formulated in terms of a creator God who has a moral purpose for creation. *Jahweh*, the god (or one god) of the ancient Hebrews, is a personal being who issues moral commands, like the Ten Commandments and the 613 statutes and ordinances of the *Torah*, the Jewish Law. Justice and mercy are commanded above all, and humans are seen as called by a personal creator to practice justice and forgiveness. Moses, who is possibly a legendary figure, standing for many now forgotten prophets, is the leading personal symbol of a faith which puts moral practice as the most important thing in life, and hopes for a future of justice and peace for the world. There are many dead ends and strange byways in the development of this stream of thought, and the recorded history of the Jewish people, in the Hebrew Bible, is quite open about the failures and sometimes unpleasantly nationalistic turns that Hebrew religion took. Despite that, there is a golden thread running through the tradition, found at its best in some of the later chapters of the Book of the prophet Isaiah, which calls on humans to revere justice and seek a way of loving and caring for even those who are enemies of the good. One main lesson of this tradition is that you cannot have spirituality without a real and practical concern for justice and peace. The world has to be changed for the better, and God commands humans to change it, promises that it can be done, and can give the strength to get it done.

There are many offshoots of the Abrahamic tradition in religion. Christianity finds in the person of Jesus one who was even more than a prophet, and was seen by his followers as somehow expressing the nature of God as love in his own life, and giving his life in order to unite humans to God. Islam finds in the Holy Qur'an a physical manifestation of the living wisdom of God, which brings God's prophetic and morally challenging revelation to fulfilment, and opens the Jewish Law, completed as the *Shariah*, to the whole world.

It is possible to focus just on the interminable arguments between these members of the same religious family, and turn away in disgust. But it is also possible to see these as different paths to a closer union with God, the ultimate spiritual reality. As such, each of them can have something of value to teach. Perhaps we can only get a hint of the nature of spiritual reality when we can appreciate more fully all of these paths (though we have just not got time to do that properly in this life). They are like imaginative visions of the spiritual. They use different images and commend different particular ways of life. But at their heart is the vision of the spiritual as a personal, just, merciful, and loving reality, which invites humans to imitate it in goodness and eventually, perhaps be united with it in love. To understand a part of a religious tradition well is to learn more about what the wisest and best of humans have discerned of Spirit, and what they have to teach.

The second great stream of religious thought originates in India. It does not interpret the spiritual in terms of one creator God. Rather, it sees personality as a rather restricted view of an infinite and all-including reality, which, in Sanskrit is called '*Brahman*' (not *Brahma*, who is a particular god). *Brahman* is the Self of All, and is sometimes described as '*Sat-Cit-Ananda*' – reality, intelligence, and bliss. It is beyond the personal, and it is the one ultimate reality which includes all other realities within itself. The goal of the spiritual quest is to pass beyond the sense that your little ego is the centre of the universe, and become conscious that at the deepest level you are one with the universal Spirit. You have to pass beyond self to unity with the Self of All, of which you are always part, though most people fail to realise that, because they live their lives in a world of illusion and attachment to trivial things. It is in meditation that you may find that sense of unity with a greater reality. It is in a life of universal compassion for all sentient beings and of indifference to the demands of the ego that you may find spiritual fulfilment.

Most Hindus in practice revere one major god – but a 'god' like *Krishna* or *Shiva* is often understood as a symbolic representation of one aspect of the Infinite Real, rather than a personal creator of the universe. It is impossible to generalise about Indian religions, as there are thousands of different sects or movements. But it is characteristic of most Indian religious thought to focus on union with a supra-personal reality which may be expressed in many different names and forms, but with which all things are one at the truest level of reality. A guru or spiritual teacher is one who can lead you 'from the unreal to the real, from darkness to light, from death to life'[21], and the way of meditation, reverence for all life, and the overcoming of selfish attachment, while being different from the Abrahamic way of obedience to divine moral commands, is a profound path of self-discovery and enlightenment.

The Indian stream divides into two main forms, both of which distinguish between the reality of *Sat-Cit-Ananda* and the world of *maya* or sensory experience. One, which is associated with Sankara and with traditional (*Hinayana*) Buddhism, regards the sensory world as illusory and to be dispelled or liberated from. When Enlightenment is achieved, you pass beyond sensory experience and individuality, and are enfolded in the One. This is not non-existence, but it is a passing-over into a higher form of existence, *Nirvana*. That higher form is infinite bliss and knowledge, but there is no longer any sense of separate individuality, and the liberated state is beyond description.

The other form is associated with Ramanuja and with more devotional forms of religious practice. It sees *maya* not as illusion but as 'play' or joyful manifestation of the One Real, in some traditions called the 'dance of *Shiva*'. All things are *Brahman*, but they are diverse manifestations of *Brahman*, which have their own form of reality, and devotion (*bhakti*) and relationship are important self-expressions of the One, which willed to 'become many', and is always manifested in diversity, while including all diversity in itself, not – like the Abrahamic God – existing apart from creation.

The third major stream of religious thought is the East Asian stream. It is found in forms of Taoism and Chinese and Japanese religion, and of 'greater vehicle' (*Mahayana*) Buddhism. Its characteristic feeling is well expressed in the saying of the Buddhist sage Buddhaghosa, '*Nirvana* is *Samsara*'. That is, there is only one reality, and liberation is to be found by seeing this one world rightly, freed from illusion. *Nirvana*, the liberated state, is not different from *Samsara*, the wheel of suffering and rebirth, but it is the very same world seen with a liberated and non-attached eye. The spiritual path is one of liberation, but it is not a renunciation of the world. It is a way of self-cultivation which leads to release from hatred, greed, and ignorance, and this occurs within the world. In Chinese forms, it is often seen as a way of harmony and balance, and being in tune with the rhythms of the cosmos (*yin* and *yang*).

One way to see all these spiritual paths is to see them as ways of approaching Spirit whose contours have been shaped by specific cultures and histories. These have laid down the basic metaphors and symbols in which enlightened and liberated spiritual guides have taught. It would, I think, be spiritually unenlightened to think that one way was completely true, and that all the others were completely false and spiritually useless. It is more likely that truth may be sought by many paths, and the best way is to seek what is positive and what makes for peace, moral action, and mental balance and maturity, in various traditions one comes across. Some find themselves able to live and practice in more than one path. Some commit themselves to one path, but still learn from others things that their preferred path has underemphasised or neglected. Some will take from a number of paths what is helpful, but not wish to be called adherents of any specific religion.

It is not sensible to say that every religion is equally good or true, and it is not sensible either to reject totally the teachings of the greatest spiritual teachers in human history. We are lucky to live in a world where we can learn from many paths, and we can discriminate between what is psychologically unhealthy and socially harmful in religion, and what makes for maturity, balance, social justice, friendship and peace. Just as it is good to learn to appreciate music, and discriminate good from bad, so it is good to learn from the spiritual insights of those who have devoted their lives to the search for liberation from selfishness and hatred and to discovering a way of union with Spirit. In the rich and diverse spirituality of today's world, we must each pursue our own path towards spiritual maturity. As we consider the wisdom of those who have done that before us, religion can be a resource for spiritual insight that we would be foolish to neglect. Religion may often seem to consist of congealed systems of once-fresh spiritual insights. But it will repay the effort to try to recover those insights – and possibly also to discover that some religious systems are not quite as congealed as they may at first seem.

11.

THE DEVELOPMENT OF RELIGION

Towards belief in one supreme spiritual reality

We may find that as religious reflection develops, many diverse apprehensions of underlying realities of emotional significance and moral purpose begin to be integrated by the thought that reality is one, and that many apparently diverse and local values are signs of something more universal and closely integrated. Instead of saying that there are many different values of beauty and goodness, all these values come to be seen as aspects of one reality. Different values are different expressions of one coherent and unitary reality of goodness and beauty. That spiritual reality will be of immense power and value, since it is the source of all the values that are perceived in experience.

Once you have got to one spiritual reality of immense value, the postulate made by people like Anselm that spiritual reality is not just of immense but of the greatest possible value ('that than which no greater can be thought') is a bold hypothesis which has the virtues of simplicity and elegance, and which is proposed as having the greatest possible integrating power. If that turns out to be true, the concept of God, of *Brahman*, of *Tao* or of the Buddha nature, will be supremely rational. If you care about rationality, that is excellent evidence for its truth, at least in a rather general sense.

Just as with materialism, the evidence for the existence of a spiritual reality of immense value does not lie directly in the occurrence of bare and relatively isolated experiences. It lies in the intellectual power of general interpretations of the whole of experience. Obviously some experiences are more important than others. In the materialist case, experiences of the success of scientific predictions will be important. But the real driving force of materialism will be the desire to achieve a unitary and integrating interpretation of all experience, one that goes well beyond the occurrence of any specific experiences. In the idealist case, experiences of beauty and moral obligation will be important – and the down-grading of them by materialists will be thought unacceptable and unfortunate. The real driving force of idealism, in other words, is the same desire for a unitary and integrating interpretation of all experience that drives materialist philosophies.

Materialism and idealism are cousins. They both start from experience, but find that a very crude empiricist account (that what you experience is reality as it is – what is often called 'naive realism') is rationally inadequate. They both look for comprehensiveness, coherence, integrating and uniting power. They both propose bold speculative hypotheses which claim to be rational interpretations of reality.

The difference is not that materialists have an obvious truth, whereas idealists add on superfluous additions. There are deep philosophical questions - questions about consciousness, value, purpose, truth, and the intelligibility of being - at issue. Both materialism and idealism are unobvious, from a viewpoint that sticks with bare experience. They are philosophical, rational, interpretations of experience. There is no neutral way of choosing between them. But a choice has to be made. Even a refusal to engage in such bold interpretations is a choice. From the point of view of both materialists and idealists, such a refusal is a decision for an unreflective life. So idealism is at worst on an intellectual par with materialism and with scepticism about reason. At best, it is an option which decides in favour of the dignity and unique value of human personhood, the intrinsic value of artistic creativity, moral freedom and responsibility, and rational understanding. It gives priority to mind, intelligence, and responsible agency. It sees them as the basis and purpose of existence, rather than as accidental by-products of blind physical processes. It expresses a decision for the intrinsic value of personal existence.

The sense of human estrangement

These thoughts about the philosophy of idealism and about the possibility of an axiological explanation for the universe can lead to the idea of a cosmic mind which is itself of supreme value, and which creates or generates the universe as the locus for the generation of many new and distinctive values. Many of these values are realised and appreciated by created finite minds, which in this way share in the self-unfolding of the potentialities of the divine Mind. There is a synergy of finite and divine actions and experiences, as the divine Mind acts in and through created minds, and takes their experiences into its own all-including experience.

However, it is all too obviously the case that finite minds often resist the divine Mind and its striving to realise forms of goodness through them. They turn aside, and in hatred, greed, and ignorance of their own natures they cut themselves off from the root of their own being. Even as we begin to suspect the existence of Supreme Mind, we also become aware that we are estranged from knowledge of it and desire for union with it. Keener awareness of God and of the demands of morality only makes us more aware of our ignorance of Supreme Beauty and of our moral failures. As we accumulate evidence for God, it also becomes evidence of our lack of knowledge and love of God.

That is where religion often comes into the picture. For all its manifest moral failures and intellectual absurdities, religious thought is rooted in a sense of human estrangement from truth and goodness, and in a search for liberation from this estrangement. It seems odd to say that our sense of the absence of God, and of lack of meaning and value in existence, is evidence for God. And yet a sense of absence can be a sense that there is something missing, something that should be there, even something that is there, but is obscured from view and hard to find.

Take, for instance, the first Holy Truth of Buddhism, that 'all is *dukkha*', suffering or unsatisfactoriness. Human life should be joyful, surrounded by beauty, filled with friendship, suffused with awe and wonder. But it is so often miserable, surrounded by ugliness, filled with hatred, and suffused with lassitude and ennui. We may begin a day with firm resolution to do creative things and build positive relationships, and yet end that day with nothing achieved, and having quarrelled with almost everyone. It is not just that things are bad; they are worse than they should be. They are corrupted and disordered. Jean-Paul Sartre put it so well: humans desire to be Gods, but this is a useless and impossible passion, and there seems no escape from useless striving for ultimately pointless objectives.

In moments of reflection, we can feel that we are in the grip of passions we cannot control and destructive forces we cannot contain. Yet this is not how human life should be, and occasionally we have glimpses of a life that is better, freer, and fuller. Philosophers have characterised this as a sense of 'Angst' or even of 'Nausea', of deep anxiety in the face of an emptiness that we seem to have created for ourselves.[22]

Of course none of this is positive evidence that there is meaning. It is evidence that we long for a meaning that we mostly cannot find, but that seems proper to us. It breeds an existential discontent and a longing for something that could restore some sense of worthwhile purpose and enduring value to existence. It is evidence for the unsatisfactoriness of the lives we lead, and of our deep longing for something better. Just as thirst is evidence of a lack which water would fill, so our sense of estrangement is evidence of a lack which only a life in relation to objective and life-fulfilling value would fill. But neither, of course, is evidence that there actually is water, or objective value.

It is as we think of the postulate of Idealism, of a life fulfilled in the realisation and appreciation of enduring values, enfolded by a love which cares for our good and is able to assure it, together with our knowledge of our actual lives, that Idealism may become, not just a possible theory, but an object of fervent desire. There may be something that would renew our lives, and indeed there are some who claim to have found it, and their lives have been transformed. All around us, in the tragic history of the world, and in our own lives, there is evidence that humans, who should rejoice in knowledge of truth, beauty, and goodness, are trapped in ignorance, ugliness and evil. It is in the tension between what we aspire to and what we are that we may find intimations of a way of life that will free us to become what we should be. The search for God or for something like God will no longer be a matter of dispassionate speculation. It will become a matter of life and death, of either remaining in a way that leads to despair and self-destruction, or (as the Danish writer Kierkegaard put it) of holding fast to 'an objective uncertainty, held fast through appropriation with the most passionate inwardness',[23] risking all by venturing into largely unknown waters in the hope that this will lead to liberation and fulfilment.

This is not evidence, in the sense of conclusive proof of some theoretical hypothesis. But it is evidence – reason for thinking – that human life lies precariously balanced between despair and hope, and that theoretical speculation will not tip the scales one way or the other. It is reason for thinking that sometimes passionate commitment must precede theoretical certainty, and that the deepest motivations of human life transcend purely rational considerations. It is not irrational to grasp at a lifebelt even if we are not sure if it will float, if otherwise we know that we will surely drown. An existential awareness of human being as poised between noble aspiration and inevitable failure gives good reason for choosing the option of life even where objective uncertainty is unobtainable. This is where we should say, perhaps, that it is not reasonable only to believe what we have good theoretical or empirical evidence for. There is good reason to seek liberation and fuller life even when the possibility of success seems small and cannot be proven, if the alternative is despair. The materialist will say that we should not believe illusions just for the sake of psychological comfort. We should take the more heroic course, and face up to despair with courage and defiance. But can we be sure that despair is the final truth about human life? Or is it evidence that something has gone fundamentally wrong with our lives, something that can be remedied by commitment to hope? There is evidence, but it is ambiguous. It is not dispassionate reason alone that will determine how we interpret the evidence. It is a much deeper decision about a fundamental choice of how we are to exist as human persons.

12.

---·eee·---

SPIRITUAL VALUES IN PERSONAL EXPERIENCE

The sense of spiritual presence

After this discussion of the sorts of evidence or argument that can properly be used to justify different sorts of human beliefs, the ground has been prepared for a discussion of the most important sort of evidence there is for belief in a supreme spiritual reality. There is such evidence, but it is not publicly accessible, universally agreed, or conclusively demonstrated by sense-observation alone. And it is none the worse for that! Spiritual belief, perhaps for most people, is based on the occurrence of particular sort of experiences, but those experiences are very personal, and they will not convince everyone beyond reasonable doubt.

We can see how evidence of this sort for believing would have to be rather special. It is not just a matter of thinking there is a supernatural person who might be observed from time to time. It is a matter of loving that which is supremely valuable, seeking to carry out objective purposes of great value, and uniting one's will to a higher will. None of these things depend upon there being some supernatural writing in the sky. They are not matters of dispassionately observed physical evidence. They are discernments of value, commitments to moral goals, and attitudes of open-ness to personal or quasi-personal features of experience. They involve claims about the objective existence of values, of goals, and of a personal dimension to what is experienced. But such claims are not value-neutral, and they do not depend upon the occurrence of peculiar though indisputable physical events which 'prove' that there is a supernatural being at work. The sort of evidence required lies in experiences which invite humans to love and obey, to know and feel the presence of spiritual reality, even or especially in the everyday events of ordinary human life.

All knowledge begins with experience. But, as I have been at pains to stress, experience is not just a matter of passively receiving sense-impressions. It is much more complex. Firstly, we need to apply concepts to interpret our sense-impressions, and these concepts, when they are fully developed, are meant to form a consistent, elegant, comprehensive, coherent, and practically useful framework which enables us to find our way around in the world. Secondly, we also need feeling responses to enable us to apprehend and evaluate our sense-experiences as pleasant or painful, as beautiful or ugly. Thirdly, these things are conditioned by a personal viewpoint and way of life, partly taught in our culture and partly developed by our own personal histories, which will influence the way we see and respond to experiences.

So human experience is a complex involving perceptions, concepts, feelings, and social and personal history. It is not surprising that people's experiences are sometimes very different, and that there can be gulfs of understanding between diverse individuals and societies. Throughout many different cultures, and in all sorts of temperaments, however, many people would claim to have a spiritual sense, a sense of transcendence, an apprehension of something that underlies experiences but is mediated in and through them, especially in some significant things, places, and events.

The spiritual sense is a non-sensory apprehension of a spiritual (non-physical) reality which is worth-while and desirable for its own sake, awareness of which evokes, or better, which is communicated by means of, feelings of reverence, worship, and love, and which inspires active response to seek it and know it and embody it in one's own personal life more fully.

I have spoken of this sense as 'personal or quasi-personal'. I mean that it is often, while being unique, rather like the awareness many people have of other people's thoughts and feelings. Even when awareness of other people's thoughts and feelings is mediated through their language and bodily behaviour, to many of us it seems that there is more that we know than just what they say and how they behave. There is a personal presence that is mediated in and through such things, that can be discerned in different ways and to different degrees by different observers.

To some people, other persons are little more than objects to be manipulated or used. But many people are more empathetic, and seem able to understand the minds of people in a much fuller way. They can understand how other people see things, what they feel, and what their values and goals are. Understanding requires empathy. Usually each of us can only understand a few people in this way, people of whom we say that they are 'kindred spirits'. Other people, outside this circle, can appear as almost total mysteries to us.

Especially when we love another person, we see in them what no one else can see in the same way. But this is not just some subjective reaction of our own. It is a real discernment. There is something that is there that perhaps only we can see. That 'seeing' is partly a function of our own views, feelings, values, and goals, and of the way in which they may resonate with those of others. This is 'involved' knowing, which means that we see only what we have made ourselves able to see.

This is not an obvious process. Love can be blind, and conceal from us many truths about others. Yet the right sort of love can open up to us aspects of others that are concealed from most people. There is no formula for finding the right sort of loving attention and perception which is not deluded by unreasonable infatuation. There is no neutral and public test for when we have achieved a true understanding others. Yet this sort of knowledge, which involves understanding and love, is one of the most important things in human existence.

You can think of awareness of the presence of Spirit in a similar way. It might not be a particular describable and distinct experience. It could be more like a general quality of awareness that there is a personal or mind-like dimension to all experience. Such awareness would have rather similar elements to those involved in the discernment of the inner personal lives of others. It is because it is similar but not quite the same that I call it 'quasi-personal'. Its intensity and quality can vary, sometimes disappearing entirely and sometimes being very obvious. But it would be a background to all experience, like apprehending the reality of mind as underlying all appearances, but as expressed variously in different particular bits of experience.

If one fairly common form of human experience seems to be of a spiritual reality which underlies all experience, but is expressed differently in different sectors of experience, then the idea of an eternal and necessary source of all being which is of supreme value and beauty and which is the often hidden depth of all experience, can seem to be an appropriate description of the object of that experience.

There is no question that we are here stretching the human imagination to its limit. All we can do is to try and work out in a rather tentative way a consistent and coherent idea of what seems to be a spiritual reality of overwhelming value. That idea is not just a purely intellectual exercise. For we are trying to gain some idea of what we really experience, when we think we can have some sort of conscious access to a being who is probably the creator of billions of planets, stars and galaxies.

Since such Spirit cannot be just one finite subject among others in the universe, this relationship is very different from a relation to other finite human beings. Yet there is often a sense of a responsiveness and of a guiding initiative that is sensitive to the changing features of our lives. There is a widely reported sense of a power not our own which works within to strengthen and empower, especially in times of difficulty and distress.[24] Thus Spirit is apprehended as existing beyond time and yet as participating in time (a model sometimes used is that of a playwright who has a full existence beyond the plays she writes, but can also play a part in those dramas too). Spirit is necessarily existing, loving, faithful, and just. Yet that changeless and utterly trustworthy nature is expressed in sensitive and creative responses to the ways in which humans think and act.

The Eternal unfolds its changeless nature in time, and the Infinite manifests its limitless nature in countless finite forms. It is in that sense that Spirit is both eternal and appears in time, and can be apprehended as active and responsive by minds which are receptive to it, both as mediated through physical objects and events, and by direct non-sensory apprehension. Such experiences are at the heart of much spiritual practice, and for those who have them they form the strongest form of evidence for the reality of Spirit.

Revelation and miracles

I have described 'religious experience' primarily in terms of a sense of a transcendent spiritual presence in and through finite things. Some people may be surprised that I have not said anything about the more specific sorts of religious experience that tend to occur to some religious believers. I am thinking of visions (appearances of spiritual objects in quasi-physical forms), revelations thought to come from a divine source, and feelings of providential guidance in life. I myself am a Christian, so I believe that Jesus appeared after his death to many disciples. I believe that the prophets and writers of the Scriptures were inspired by God. And I believe that many people have felt guidance in their lives which has come from God.

More generally, I believe that people all over the world, in many faiths and sometimes in none, have experienced visions, inspirations, and guidance in their lives. I know this is a problem for many people today, because they are aware that human beings are prone to suffer from delusions and hallucinations, and because such visions and inspirations often seem to conflict with one another.

Some philosophically minded scientists also say that the laws of nature do not allow miracles to happen, and we know that people tend to exaggerate miracle stories, and that no miracle has ever occurred under strictly controlled laboratory conditions. So there is a widespread scepticism about such special experiences.

Of course if you are a dogmatic materialist all alleged revelations and miracle stories are bound to be false, because there are no spiritual realities at all. But if you are more open-minded, you will not dismiss out of hand the many claims that are made that there is a spiritual dimension which sometimes makes itself known to human minds. As a matter of fact, it would be very odd if there was a spiritual dimension, and nobody ever experienced it at all. It would be even more odd if there was a personal God with a purpose for human lives, who never revealed, in what would probably be very striking and special experiences, what this purpose was.

Take miracles, for example. The Scottish philosopher David Hume set things off in a very misleading direction when he defined a miracle as 'a transgression of a law of nature by a particular volition of the Deity'.[25] This was misleading, because the very idea of a law of nature did not really exist until early modern times, and the miracles mentioned in the Bible were written down long before anybody had ever thought of laws of nature. Also the idea of a 'transgression' already makes a miracle sound like a criminal act. A less misleading definition of a miracle is: an amazing or astounding event, which transcends the natural powers of physical objects, and which has a strong spiritual content, manifesting the presence and power of spiritual reality.

There are three parts to this definition. First, a miracle is astounding. It is not only rare and unexpected. It is completely out of the ordinary and awe-inspiring. Second, it cannot be explained in terms of the normal and regular behaviour of physical objects. It does not fall under any general law, which states that this miracle is bound to happen in these situations, however infrequent they are. And third, it communicates something important about the spiritual (you might call it 'mental', though it is not human) power which has brought it about.

David Hume argued that you should never believe a miracle had happened unless it was more unlikely that the witness to it was lying or deceived, than it was that the miracle had actually occurred. For him, this meant that you should never believe a miracle had happened. For, he thought, it was always quite likely that a witness to an amazing event had been deceived, whereas the occurrence of a miracle (in his definition, an event that broke the laws of nature) was virtually impossible.

Hume is loading the dice unfairly by saying that a miracle is virtually impossible. If there is a God who created the laws of nature, for example, it would be pretty likely, indeed almost certain, that God would influence the laws of nature. It would also be likely that sometimes God's influence would cause objects to do things that went beyond the normal operation of the laws of nature. These things would not be silly or arbitrary. They would have to communicate something important about God. So, for instance, if Jesus appeared after his death to some disciples, this would communicate, in a very effective way, that death is not the end, and that Jesus truly lived with God. Does that make the resurrection likely? Not really, because it is amazing and unpredictable. But it is not irrational or impossible. With hindsight, a person might think that in the light of the Messianic prophecies in the Old Testament, and of a new revelation of God's purpose to unite human lives to the divine life, it was an entirely natural and fitting thing for God to do. A Christian would say that it is very unlikely that the disciples were lying or deceived (many of them were persecuted, and some died, for their beliefs). And the appearing of a dead man who ascends to the glory of God, is very likely indeed, given God's purpose to lead all people to divine glory with Christ. We can accept Hume's point about evidence, but be pretty sure that he was wrong in assessing the probability of miracles.

The resurrection of Jesus was an awe-inspiring event which falls under no law of nature (there is no law which says, 'Very good prophets will be raised from the dead'). And it communicates very important truths about Jesus' victory over death and about human destiny. It is a miracle, and the evidence for it is good. But – and it is a very important 'but' – the evidence is not overwhelming or felt to be compelling by everyone. Your estimate of the probability of a miracle will depend on whether or not you think there is a God. Your estimate of the probability of this miracle will depend on many of your other beliefs about God. If you think Jesus was not the promised Messiah, or if you think Christians are wrong in believing that Jesus is the human incarnation of God, that will weaken the evidence for you. On the other hand, testimony to the resurrection, plus personal experience of what you take to be the risen Lord, may be a strong contributory factor in causing you to believe that Jesus was the promised Messiah and the embodiment of the Divine Word. These are difficult and complicated matters, and it is not really surprising that there are disagreements. In other words, estimates of evidence will vary, depending upon many other related beliefs within a general world-view. In that respect, they are very like philosophical beliefs, where philosophers give different weights to the same evidence, in the light of many other beliefs they may hold (about the probability of materialism being true, for example). So while miracles are evidence, they are not overwhelmingly good evidence for everybody.

The argument that laws of nature make miracles impossible is not, on its own, a strong argument. It wholly depends on what you think laws of nature are, and whether they are in principle unbreakable. It seems very dogmatic to say that there are general laws which apply universally – even to things we never have and never will see – and which can never be broken. Strangely, David Hume thought that, as far as reason can tell, laws of nature are not necessary, so they can be broken at any time. Believers in God arguably have more faith in the laws of nature than Hume did, for they believe God will establish rational and predictable laws of physical behaviour, and can be trusted to make sure they continue to apply most of the time. Theists are also likely to think, however, that the laws of nature serve a higher spiritual purpose, and that sometimes God will make things happen that would not be caused just by laws of physical nature, but require a spiritual cause in addition. Much of this old debate can be by-passed today by the recognition that, for quantum physics, laws are probabilistic, not necessary, so there is good reason to think that the very improbable will happen from time to time (not too often, we hope). Theists, of course, think that it is God who makes miracles occur, and always for a good reason, so they are not just random freak events.

A more difficult problem, also stressed by Hume, is the fact that many reported miracles and apparent revelations are fraudulent or irrational, and that even when they are not, they often seem to conflict, so they cannot all be genuine. Yet this is not really a major problem. Human beings are subject to trickery and madness, we all know that. But that does not mean that all reports are fraudulent. We could not go on living if we did not have a fundamental trust in the testimony of others. Universal scepticism is not something we could live with. So there must be ways in which we can try to distinguish genuine from fraudulent testimonies. We normally sort these things out by enquiring into the character and track-record of people who claim inspirations or visions, and by asking whether their reports fit into, or are at least consistent with, the world-view we have already formed. So, for instance, alleged visions which are used to generate large amounts of money are not very convincing in this respect. Reports of UFO abductions are generally doubted, because of the oddity of thinking that aliens from many light years away have travelled to earth just to poke about in secret, in rural areas of the USA, and in the smellier areas of human bodies, rather than contacting some reputable authorities. In other words, we should not dogmatically assert that miracles cannot happen. We should ask about the credentials of the witnesses, about whether there seem to be good, spiritually important, reasons for the occurrence of the alleged miracle, and about whether the miracle fits into a general and plausible world-view that we accept.

With regard to conflicts of belief, we need to remember that human interpretations of particular experiences are almost always governed by a more general scheme of beliefs which are already held. Roman Catholics tend to have visions of the Virgin Mary, Buddhists have visions of a compassionate *Bodhisattva* (a saviour-Buddha), and Hindus have visions of Krishna. The schemes of belief within which such visions occur differ, and the visions take on the colouring of those schemes. It seems very reasonable to say that what appears is a spiritual presence taking the visual form of a figure familiar to the devotees in question. Few people, after all, would say that the Blessed Virgin, who, Christians believe, has been absorbed into the divine life, really looks just as she appears in visions to human beings. Visions, and thoughts too, take a form which is accessible to particular humans at a particular stage in a particular historically developing culture. They do not simply over-ride human thoughts and beliefs, but shape them by an inward spiritual influence.

So I think that miracles, claims to inspiration and spiritual guidance, do form an important part of the evidence for God or Spirit. They are not going to be infallible, conclusive, and free from ambiguity. They are not going to be accepted as good evidence by everybody. They are perhaps for the few, rather than for the many, though many people have some inkling of such experiences. However, if those experiences are not successfully embedded in a more general and roughly coherent world-view they are liable to be placed in the margins of consciousness and ignored.

For many people appeal to miracles and special experiences of inspiration are too controversial to be taken as good evidence. But there is a type of human experience of the spiritual which is less bound up with the often controversial claims made by specific religions, and which is nevertheless evidence for a spiritual reality. That is the non-sensory apprehension of a seemingly transcendent reality which occurs to many human beings, whether they would call themselves religious or not. These 'apprehensions of spirit' are a frequent part of human experience. But is it reasonable to accept them as giving authentic awareness of the nature of reality?

Apprehensions of spirit

There is nothing very peculiar in the thought of non-sensory apprehension. Our sense-organs transmit information to our brains, and it is the firing of neurons in parts of our brains that causes us to have sensations of various sorts. We know that we can have sensations without our sense-organs being employed, in dreams and imagination, for instance. So it does not seem impossible to have seeming apprehensions of things that are not caused by sense-organs.

Neuro-scientists have discovered many astounding facts about how the human brain functions. They are close to locating which physical structures in the brain need to be working properly for consciousness, and for logical and moral thought, to be possible. Some have claimed to be able to generate 'religious experiences' by stimulating the brain with electro-magnetic pulses.[26] Such claims are hotly disputed, but they are not in principle difficult for believers in genuine spiritual apprehensions to accept. Neuro-scientists can cause people to form mental pictures of human faces by electrical stimulation of the facial recognition area of the brain. But that does not cause us to think that people never see genuine human faces. It just shows, fascinatingly enough, that common experiences can be artificially evoked by stimulation of neurons in the brain. This suggests that such brain-activity must occur to enable people to see faces in normal experience. So it is, presumably, with spiritual apprehensions. Relevant parts of the brain must be healthy, active, and functioning properly to enable people to have spiritual experiences. And something roughly like such experiences can be simulated by electrical interference with the brain.

Some neuro-scientists suggest that such experiences are simply physical states of the brain, without objective reality. But that by no means follows from their discoveries. In fact it is a very odd conclusion to suggest. When we see trees, mountains, and people, the relevant perceptual and cognitive areas of our brains must be working properly. But few think that there are no objective trees, mountains, and people, or that such objects are identical with some of our brain-states. It is the same with experiences of the spiritual. The fact that certain areas of our brains must be working properly for us to have such experiences does not show that there is no object that we are experiencing. On the contrary, the presumption is that, if the brain is functioning properly, its perceptions will be of genuine objects.

That spiritual apprehensions are genuine perceptions of something, however, cannot be taken for granted. If you are absolutely sure there is no spiritual reality, then of course apprehensions of it must be illusions. But it seems unduly dogmatic to be absolutely sure of something that millions of people, some of them quite intelligent I suppose, disagree with. There are some relevant tests for whether seeming apprehensions could be genuine, which parallel tests for genuine vision or hearing. In the case of the five senses, we can check eyes and ears for whether they are functioning normally. So we can in principle check the brain for whether it is functioning normally. If it is, there is some reason to think that it provides genuine information.

In the case of the five senses, we can see whether different senses corroborate each other – whether, for example, the sight of water in the desert is followed by the taste of it when we get to the oasis, or whether it disappears as we get closer to a mirage. In the case of mental apprehensions, there are no other senses to compare with it. But there are results of genuine apprehension that may be more or less practically useful and life-enhancing. So we can check whether our sense of Spirit, which should be a sense of a beautiful and inspiring reality, leads to greater courage, patience, wisdom, or what Buddhists call mindfulness. We can ask whether a spiritual sense leads to a more balanced psychology, and whether its implications are consistent with knowledge we derive from other sources, like the natural sciences. I think the answer in many cases seems to be positive. But of course we need to investigate the matter as fully as possible, allowing for many sorts of distinction that have to be made between different sorts of spiritual experiences.

In the case of the five senses, we can check whether other similarly placed people see or hear what we do. So we can check whether our experiences of Spirit are corroborated by other people. We need to bear in mind that not all people put themselves in a position that is receptive to such things, and some positively block off any possibility. The philosopher Immanuel Kant, for example, who firmly believed in God, yet denied the possibility of any special apprehensions of God. That was perhaps because he was so temperamentally opposed to a certain sort of Christians who claimed always to be talking to God and claiming to have a special route to privileged knowledge because they were specially inspired by the Spirit. There is no doubt that many claims to know supernatural entities are made by people who are known to be deluded or pathological in other ways. Such claims will naturally be subject to critical doubt. But plenty of claims to intuit some sort of spiritual reality are made by otherwise sane, wise, and informed people who are not drunk or deranged. It seems to me that if the brain is functioning well, if people become morally better or wiser after their experience, and if our apprehensions are widely corroborated by many wise, sane, and morally pre-eminent people, claims to apprehend Spirit should be taken seriously.

If there is a spiritual reality, this would be the most natural way to have a sense of it. We would 'feel' or be aware of the presence of something overwhelming beautiful and desirable. Such apprehension would not be like the unemotional registering of a fact, like seeing that there is a house in front of one. It would be strongly emotional (affective might be a better word), like seeing a person you love and are irresistibly attracted to. And it would be intrinsically motivating, moving you to desire it, to know it, imitate it, and seek to be united to it as a goal of your actions.

There is no doubt that such feelings occur, with various degrees of intensity, to millions of people. They are usually conceptually vague, even when intense. That is to say, they do not carry a specific description with them. In fact they often defeat any attempt to give a description of them, except to say that they can be more or less intense, and carry an impression of great beauty, goodness, tranquillity, and love. How they are described depends upon the general world view of specific cultures. They are not by any means all described as experiences of God. I do not find it strange to say that the Buddhist experience of Enlightenment is one variety of experience of a reality of transcendent beauty and goodness, and that the Christian experience of Christ is another. This does not mean that all descriptions will be equally true or adequate. But it does mean that there are many ways of describing what may be genuine deliverances of the spiritual sense.

Thus it is reasonable to think that there are ways of testing the genuineness of the spiritual sense. First of all, however its object is described, it must be consistent with the best well-established human knowledge of the nature of the world. Then it must pass our ordinary tests of moral goodness, and indeed be seen to go beyond ordinary moral demands to what seems a deeper level of goodness – by which I mean that such qualities as justice, compassion for the weak, and universal concern for well-being must be present in an outstanding degree. And it must contribute to personal psychological maturity, to wisdom and insight. The person who has had genuine experience of the spiritual should be wise, good, and psychologically mature. We should doubt that people who are ignorant, dangerous, and unstable, have had genuine experiences of the spiritual.

13.

----- ∞ -----

EXPERIENCE AND PERSONAL ETHICS

Testing experience

It may be said that many religious people are ignorant, dangerous and unstable, and they may claim to be genuine followers of God. But they are hardly followers of the Good, the Beautiful, and the Intelligible. What, then, have they experienced? It seems that in these cases you do have to speak of false perception. After all, the way you see and interpret all your experiences depends on your personality, on what sort of person you are and on your general values and interests.

Buddhists speak of the 'three fires' of greed, hatred, and ignorance which consume human lives. To see the Good you must be liberated from these three fires. You must be non-attached, compassionate, and wise. Only if you have such qualities will you be able to see justly. If you are blindly attached to some destructive cause or belief or self-interested pursuit; if you hate those who differ from you; and if you refuse to learn from those who understand more than you; then what you see will at least in part reflect your own short-sighted and disordered viewpoint. Any political cause you support will be a chauvinistic and short-sighted one, which perhaps seeks to oppress or destroy other nations and races, and which will have a restricted, censorial and repressive agenda. And any religious cause you support will similarly tend to be very dogmatic and exclusive, founded on hatred of heretics, and opposed to new and possibly disturbing knowledge. It would be easier if we could just ban such people from political and religious organisations. Unfortunately, they will then start their own political or religious sects, and probably regard even most other 'believers' as heretics or infidels. That is – and religious belief-systems usually stress that it is – human nature.

Within such disordered belief systems, which are widespread throughout the world, any beliefs you have about a spiritual realm are going to be so interpreted that it will be almost impossible to have a genuine apprehension of a Spirit who is goodness, beauty and rational truth. However, if you break free of these human failings, and begin to cultivate non-attachment, compassion, and wisdom, that may enable you to apprehend the objective reality in which they are supremely enshrined. Just as you begin by seeing only what your personal orientation allows you to see, so it will become increasingly the case that just perception will enable you to become more like what you see.

What you actually are governs what you can see. But as you continue to look, what you see begins to govern what you become. That is what it means to say that knowing the Good means loving the Good, which means becoming like the Good. Perhaps if we had full knowledge of the Good we would have become true participants in the Good. Apprehension, affection, and transformation of life are inextricably linked in spiritual sensibility.

Human knowledge changes and develops. Human morality does so too, and not always for the better. Beliefs about what makes for human well-being and personal fulfilment are not the same in every society. So these tests of genuineness are not infallible, and they will probably change in detail over time. It would seem to be a great mistake to judge the descriptions of what was spiritually sensed thousands of years ago by the standards of what we might say in the very different world view of the twenty first century. It is, however, illuminating to be able to trace the path we have travelled from there to here, and acknowledge where we have come from, if we are to understand more fully what we now are, and even imagine what we might yet become.

It may seem that I have suggested that those who long for goodness, wisdom, and love, will have spiritual experiences. In general, I believe this to be true. But what about those who desperately long to know God, for example, but do not have any sense of the divine presence? One possibility is that people are looking for the wrong thing, for an experience of God literally speaking to them, perhaps. Such experiences do occur, but they may be rather rare. What is normally to be expected, if idealism is true, is a more general affective belief that all is founded on a mind-like, beautiful and intelligible reality. If held genuinely, such a belief will of itself have a marked effect on the attitudes and feelings of the believer, but not necessarily in the form of distinct and deeply moving experiences.

Some great spiritual writers, like John of the Cross, speak of a 'dark night of the soul', when even those who seek to love God are without any strong sense of divine presence. In such cases, it may be that they are entering into the general human experience of alienation from Spirit, and this is part of their spiritual development. John of the Cross's writings show that even in the 'dark night', he was in fact able to recollect past experiences of the spiritual, and continued to have a firm hope for a closer conscious union with the spiritual. What may be lacking at many times is any sense of refreshment, comfort, and beatitude. That, for some, may be part of the way to the wisdom which eventually makes a stronger sense of spiritual presence possible.

The ascent from the cave

While idealists believe that all reality is a manifestation of mind, they also usually believe that this reality is hidden behind a veil of ignorance and appearance. In Plato's allegory of the Cave,[27] in his dialogue 'The Republic', people are chained in a deep cave, and see not real things, but only the shadows of puppets flickering on the inner wall of the cave. In the Indian tradition of *Advaita Vedanta* (non-dualism) humans are imprisoned in a world of illusions, and need to train by disciplined meditation and moral practice to achieve the insight that they are in fact parts of a greater unitary reality of *sat-cit-ananda*, being, intelligence, and bliss, the Self of All. Humans are trapped in the illusions of selfishness and desire, and the ascent to just vision is an ascent of the soul to the divine. This ascent may be long and arduous, though for some rare souls it seems miraculously instantaneous and complete. For most of us, however, estrangement from the Good is the initial position, and we need to grow in patience and courage, to learn commitment without consolation, and perhaps even to suffer misfortune at the hands of others, before we are in a position to see reality with a purified spiritual sensibility.

Without some sense of spiritual presence, without some extraordinarily intense apprehensions by outstanding individuals, and without the hope of a fuller apprehension of the Good and the Beautiful, the one self-existent reality, the infinite and eternal, idealism might be a rather abstract speculation about the nature of reality. I myself would still find it irresistibly attractive, elegant, and plausible. But the experience of life as a journey from greed, hatred, and ignorance to union with a reality of self-giving love and supremely rational wisdom, and the spiritual 'sense and taste of the infinite' (as the eighteenth century German theologian Friedrich Schleiermacher called it), or of felt total dependence upon a reality of supreme goodness and beauty, provides evidence for the existence of Spirit which is completely compelling for those who experience it.

Claims to personal experience without the rational backing of something like idealist philosophy and the conviction that there is a consistent and coherent idea of Spirit, might be set aside as purely subjective aberrations. Idealist philosophy without personal apprehensions of spirit by many of the wisest and holiest of human beings might be rejected as just one rational but inconclusive possibility among others. Take the two together, and the evidence for the dependence of our common sense world upon a deeper mind-like reality of beauty and supreme value becomes very strong.

Naturally, to accept that evidence as the basis for a firm commitment to knowing and realising the Good is a matter of faith. But that faith is not 'believing without evidence'. It is committing oneself to a belief which is well but not conclusively evidenced (nothing in this area is conclusive), largely because it seems strongest in terms of its moral attraction and its contribution to human well-being. There are no doubt many forms of faith, and some of them are evil and irrational. This should not prevent us seeing that there is a form of faith in the Good, the Beautiful, and the True, in their objective existence, and in the possibility of their realisation in human lives, which is both morally inspiring and fully rational.

TWO CONCEPTS OF RATIONALITY

Evidentialist reasoning and Clifford's rule

I began by claiming that, contrary to what some people say, there is such a thing as good evidence for the existence of a spiritual reality. I then tried to analyse what is meant by 'evidence', and in particular what could constitute evidence for a spiritual reality of supreme value. I suggested that it is misleading to accept a common-sense view of the world and then ask if there is evidence for the existence of some extra being outside that world. The real question is about the nature of the world as we experience it. The question at issue is whether this world is a world just of physical objects, with human persons as very complex physical objects, or whether the world also possesses a spiritual or mind-like dimension, or indeed whether the world is in its essential being spiritual or mind-like.

Looking for evidence to answer this question is not a matter of simple observation or of carrying out experiments. It is not a scientific or observational issue. It is a matter of interpretation and evaluation, of trying to understand our experience in the best way. I considered six main areas of human experience – the arts, morality, philosophy, science, religion, and personal (non-sensory) experience. In each area I found that there were deep disputes and apparently unresolvable differences of interpretation. But there was plenty of evidence for seeing, in each area (even in science, insofar as the 'material' is seen as an expression of an underlying mathematical reality) a non-sensory and non-material aspect of reality which is more than but expressed in and through, the physical world. This 'spiritual sense' is either an imaginary projection of human desires and ideals onto objective reality, or a discernment of values and ideals which are really and objectively there. There are no observations, experiments, or decisive reasons, for deciding which interpretation to take. But just as there is evidence for a 'naturalist' view which seems compelling to many, so also there is evidence for a 'spiritual' view which seems compelling to many. And that spiritual view of reality can be elegantly, coherently, and fruitfully stated – and has been by many philosophers throughout the ages.

The idea that there are inherently unresolvable disputes about evidence, and the idea that evidence can be strong only for people who have other supporting background beliefs, may be felt to be so unpalatable that such evidence may simply be ignored. All proper evidence, it may be said, should be open to anyone and should be publicly testable by experiment. We can get this sort of evidence in normal science and in everyday experience. Why don't we just stick to that, and leave these other tricky sorts of evidence alone? The only acceptable form of reasoning, according to this view, is evidentialist reasoning – all our beliefs must be based on evidence of a rather narrow sensory, publicly accessible, indisputable sort. If they are not, they are not reasonable.

Such a view of evidence is neatly summed up in a well-known quote from the humanist thinker W. K. Clifford: 'It is wrong always, everywhere, and for anyone, to believe anything upon insufficient evidence' ('The Ethics of Belief', in *Contemporary Review*, 1877)[28]. The irony is that this resounding statement, taken by some to be a statement of what it is to be rational, is itself fairly obviously irrational. Would any rational person think that it is wrong for a six year old child to believe what he is told by his parents, even though the child has no evidence about the matter, and his parents may not have any either? What his parents say may be mistaken. But what would be wrong would be for the child to reject what he was told, since that would amount to accusing his parents of lying. Clifford's principle needs to be qualified so that it only applies to mature, reasonable and well-informed persons who are capable of assessing evidence for themselves. That may seem to be a small qualification, but it actually takes a lot of work and a good deal of maturity and training to become such a person. Perhaps there are not so many people who qualify.

Moreover, it is not clear what is meant by having sufficient evidence for a belief. Do I have to have the evidence myself? That would mean I had to know all about history, quantum mechanics, philosophy, and psychology, and many other things. That requirement is totally unrealistic. So do I just have to believe that someone else has sufficient evidence, because of their expertise and experience? It probably does, but I will often have to believe they have such expertise on authority (because someone tells me they have). I am in no position to quiz them on their expertise myself. So even accepting a belief because we think there is sufficient evidence for it often involves trust in the expertise and honesty of some authority. That is another huge qualification to what we might call Clifford's rule.

It is not even absolutely clear what is meant by 'evidence'. One standard interpretation of evidence would be the case of a detective finding footprints in the snow, leading to a dead body. The footprints and the body are publicly observable physical data, and of course the owner of the shoes is an observable physical person. Such evidence need not be conclusive, and indeed it is often the case that you need several pieces of rather poor evidence which together form a cumulative case for identifying the murderer. But the footprints become evidence by using a process of inference. You know from experience that people usually wear shoes, that the prints can tell you what sort and size of shoe made the prints, that the suspect wore just such shoes, that there was no one else around at the time, and, if you are lucky, that he has a pair of shoes with just the right sort of mud on them.

You are assuming the reliability of memory, knowledge of what usually happens, assuming that causal laws remain constant, and trying to eliminate other possible causes, to get the causal narrative down to one main possibility. Evidence in such a case relies on there being causal regularities between physical events, and on the mind being a reliable observer of such regularities.

Reliable observation cannot be taken for granted – people in criminal cases very often claim to see things that never happened, or fail to see things that did happen. People are not very reliable, though some people have to be trusted to some extent, and a lot can turn on whether they are reliable or not. Also, some observations require detailed technical knowledge, like the knowledge that people have unique DNA prints, and the knowledge of how to identify chunks of DNA.

So what is required for good evidence is competent and reliable observation, preferably tested by lots of experimental work, the existence of regular causal connections between physical events, and of course the existence of some physically observable data that can make one possible causal narrative more plausible than others.

What makes a piece of evidence sufficient? Again, there is a standard, but restricted, definition, which is often used in English law. It is that sufficient evidence is evidence which puts the guilt of a suspect beyond reasonable doubt. If the evidence suggests that a particular owner of size 9 leather boots is guilty of murder, but a good lawyer can make you think that the owner might have lent his boots to a friend on the night in question, you may have a reasonable doubt about his guilt. You will have to let him go.

If you accept these two rather restricted, but quite common, definitions, and seek to apply Clifford's rule, you will have to say this: it is absolutely wrong, in all circumstances whatsoever, to believe anything that is not a matter of the absolutely reliable observation of some physically observable data that are caused by regular, repeated, and well-established causal processes. Moreover, that observation and that process of inference must put the belief beyond any reasonable doubt.

There are, fortunately, plenty of cases like that. That the sun rises every morning in the East, that if I fall from a high building I will die, or that smoking causes lung cancer, are all such cases (though the last one is still disputed by some), and there are thousands of others. We could not live without having such beliefs. They are all based on experience and common sense inference, and without such beliefs we would not survive very long. The question is whether all our beliefs have to be like that. Could we even survive successfully if we believed nothing except things of that sort?

I think it is perfectly obvious that we could not. The most obvious case is the case of moral beliefs. We believe, I hope, that we should be kind to others, that we should not kill the innocent, and that we should be fair. Some observations are relevant to such beliefs – we must know what killing is, and what the consequences of killing are, and whether people like to be killed or not. But even after all the data are in, people may disagree about whether it is ever right to kill the innocent. Observable evidence will not settle the matter. We can never settle it beyond reasonable doubt, though we can construct reasons both for killing the innocent (usually in extreme circumstances, like killing them when they ask us to do so) and against killing the innocent (if human life is of absolute value in itself). It is just a fact that people will differ on whether they think such reasons are sufficient or not. There is no neutral way of settling the issue.

You could always take the heroic course of refusing to say that we have any moral beliefs, but that just seems perverse. It seems much better to say that we have lots of moral beliefs, that experience and argument are important in forming them, but that they are neither based solely on publicly observable causal sequences nor ever established beyond reasonable doubt. There are no doubt ways of forming moral beliefs sensibly or rationally, but they will not obey Clifford's rule (taken in its restricted sense).

Clifford could always reply that he was only talking about factual beliefs, and moral beliefs, whatever they are, are not factual. We have now begun to qualify the rule. It is not about all beliefs, after all, but only about factual beliefs. But that raises the question: is it only about one sort of factual beliefs? Most people think there are lots of perfectly ordinary factual beliefs that also break Clifford's rule, and cause us no difficulty.

A very clear example is beliefs about my dreams. It is not wrong for me to believe that last night I dreamed I was in the Bahamas. I did, and I am sure that I did, and however hard you hammer me on the head with Clifford's rule, I am more sure that I had that dream than I am that Clifford's rule is sensible.

I cannot prove that my observation of my dream was reliable. Some really tough-minded philosophers say that I could not have observed any dream, because there are no inner mental events at all. Others may say that I only have my memory to go on, and memory is notoriously unreliable, so I may just be having a false memory of what went on in the night. All I have to go on is that I remember dreaming. I cannot even prove it to myself, because I cannot get back into my dream to check whether I really had it. Nobody else saw it, and I just think I saw it. So I cannot prove that anybody saw it, or even that there was really anything to see. But if you tell me that, I will get very annoyed. Because I just know I saw it. But the fact is, it is certainly not beyond reasonable doubt.

My dream was not physically observable – I did not have my eyes open, and nobody else could see it. It was not part of a repeated causal process. The description of the state, 'I am dreaming of the Bahamas', is not part of any causal sequence. Even if the dream was caused by eating too much cheese, there is no causal law known to man that says, 'If you eat X amount of cheese, you will dream of the Bahamas'.

So here is a belief I have – 'I dreamed I was in the Bahamas' – which is not reliably observed, not even physically observable, not part of any regular causal sequences from which the event could be reliably inferred, and not beyond reasonable doubt. Yet it is not wrong for me to believe it. So there must be something wrong with Clifford's rule.

Dreaming is only one of a huge class of mental events that I directly know by introspection, by looking into my own mind. Feeling, thinking, imagining, even seeing, hearing, and touching, are things I strongly believe to exist, but do not fit into a restrictive definition of 'sufficient evidence'. I am aware, of course, that philosophers argue hugely about all these topics. But that only strengthens my point – they argue about them, and there is no way of resolving their arguments to the universal agreement of all competent arguers. So putting things beyond reasonable doubt cannot be a condition of reasonable belief – at least if philosophers are thought to be reasonable.

Problems with Clifford's rule

What we need to do is get a less restricted interpretation of Clifford's rule. That is easily done. We probably still want to relate evidence to experience in quite a strong way. There must be a starting-point in experience for reasonable beliefs. As the British empiricist philosophers used to say, 'All knowledge begins with experience', and I have repeatedly said that I am inclined to agree with that. But not all experience is of publicly observable objects which are parts of regular causal processes. The experience of my dreams and thoughts is not experience of publicly observable objects, but it is experience of something that exists, and that I can reasonably believe to exist merely by having the experience or even (as in the case of dreams) merely by remembering such an experience.

Even when we do have beliefs about publicly observable objects, those objects may not be parts of regular causal sequences, and we may not be able to get agreement about them. For instance, historians talk about people and events that can be publicly observed, at least in theory (if we had been there, perhaps). But there are no 'laws of history', by which we could measure the speed or weight of historical events and make predictions about them. We are dealing with people, their motives, desires, and values. These are not measurable, and we cannot put them into laws except in the most vague way. Even when we try to formulate laws of human behaviour, they can always be broken – as any competent economist will testify. So there are no causal laws we can appeal to when talking about human actions (you might wish there were, or even hope there might be; but at the moment there are none).

It is also obvious that historians differ markedly about their conclusions. History would be much less interesting if they did not. I have just been reading a number of accounts of the life of the sixteenth-century English contemporary of Henry the Eighth, Thomas Cromwell. Some historians say he was an unprincipled, ruthless, evil monster. Others defend him as the strongly principled architect of a form of Parliamentary democracy in England. All these historians have the same 'evidence', in the form of historical records. But their disagreements seem irresolvable.

There are unsettlable disputes about what happened in history. Historians rarely settle things beyond reasonable doubt. It is important to note that part of the interest of history is precisely that we have different interpretations, different perspectives, on the past. These reflect differing perspectives on human life and human values, and it may be thought good to have such differing perspectives, as it increases our own understanding of human life and its diversity.

The notion of 'evidence' has now broadened out to include things that are not publicly observable, things that do not fall under scientific or regular laws, and things which are inherently unsettlable, because our beliefs about them embody personal perspectives which will never be universally shared.

It follows that if you now ask what 'sufficient' evidence is, you will have to examine the sort of thing you are talking about before you can decide what sort of evidence is sufficient to come to a reasonable conclusion. As we have seen, in common-sense everyday experience, we might want to insist on trained observations of physical objects in regular causal interaction, and on things that have been established beyond reasonable doubt. If we are flying on an aeroplane, for example, we would be wise to know that there are tested and trained experiments that put it beyond reasonable doubt that the plane will not fall out of the air.

Even in that case we would not need to have the evidence ourselves, or even know how to get it reliably. There is a lot of room for trust. So we often have to trust that other people have such evidence, and that we can rely on their testimony. It would be silly to insist that we must gather all the evidence ourselves. This becomes especially important in physics, where we rightly trust in what expert physicists say, but we often could not possibly follow their arguments ourselves, even if they were put right under our noses.

In ethics, politics, history, in making judgments about other people, and perhaps in matters of artistic taste, too, we might be wise to put our trust in people we believe to be wise and experienced, and whom we find to be in general sympathetic to our own perspective. Some of them might have helped to shape our perspective.

It would not be wrong to do this, to rely on authorities to a great extent. In fact it would be silly and ignorant not to do so. We all have to learn, and we have to learn by trusting people who know more and are more capable in specific areas than we are.

What would be wrong would be to ignore all differing and critical perspectives, or to fail to take them seriously when they arise. As Socrates said, 'The unexamined life is not worth living', and it is our duty to understand criticisms of our beliefs when they arise, not to turn away from them in horror, but respond to them as fairly as we can. Yet, though this is true, you could hardly insist that everyone spends all their time looking for criticisms and trying to answer them. That would drive many people mad, and they would not have time or inclination to do it anyway.

It is the duty of some people to examine arguments and look for reasoned assessments of just how strong or weak they are – that is what I am doing now. But we know, if we are not stupid, that there is no one obviously correct answer to many real and important questions, and that matters are usually more complicated than people think.

The duty of most people is much less than this. It is basically to trust what they have learned from people they have reason to respect, but not to turn a blind eye to criticisms when they arise. They should not blindly insist on conforming to ancient authorities or customary beliefs even when those authorities have reasonably been challenged because of new information. They must be prepared to discern the proper limits of authority, be prepared to give a reason for their beliefs, and try to understand the arguments of opponents, and see whether their criticisms are just. They are not required to be full-time philosophers, and they can without criticism trust the views of others who share their general perspective, and who have responded in depth to counter-arguments. In other words, Clifford asks too much if he asks that you should always be calling your own beliefs in question, and trying to counter the arguments of great philosophers or scientists who disagree with you. But he is right if he says that you should not have a completely closed mind, and that you should try to find something valuable in other views than your own – though in most cases that will cause you to modify your own perspective rather than to give it up altogether. This, though important, is now so weak that it is questionable whether one should call it Clifford's – or anybody else's – rule.

After all this, what is the most reasonable thing to do with Clifford's rule? I suggest that the most reasonable thing is to completely reject it insofar as it requires that for all your beliefs you must have virtual certainty about publicly observable events that fall under strict causal laws. It is, however, a condition of being reasonable to remain as open as possible to perspectives other than one's own, to understand them as fully and sympathetically as possible, and to seek to be aware of any well-established knowledge that might cause one to modify one's own initial beliefs.

Then you could say that it is wrong to believe anything if you do not believe that someone has enough evidence to make a specific interpretation of certain kinds of experience plausible, even when that interpretation is inherently unsettlable. That may seem extremely wide, and indeed it is hard to say that it excludes anything very definite about religion or philosophy, for example. Belief in Spirit would be quite acceptable if you believed that someone was able to give a coherent idealist account of experience, and that there were confirming apprehensions of a cosmic mind, even though that account was widely disputed and those experiences were not universally shared.

For these reasons I doubt whether it is really reasonable to accept Clifford's rule. Some things do not seem to be matters of evidence at all. Pure mathematics is a case in point, but so are the sort of basic beliefs about which many philosophers fret – the belief that the future will be like the past, that physical objects exist unobserved, that other people are not zombies, or that humans have free will. Such beliefs seems to be based on what it takes to make sense of our experience, on considerations of simplicity, consistency, coherence, comprehensiveness, and practical utility. Is this 'evidence'? It is more a matter, as the philosopher Immanuel Kant said, of having a conceptual scheme which makes sense of human experience in general, more a condition of the possibility of having comprehensible experience than a piece of particular experience.

All knowledge may begin with experience, but experience contains something of an intellectual or rational nature which is not so much an object of experience, but a condition of experience. I have argued that experience also contains points of transcendence at which some reality can be discerned by those who are open to it, which goes beyond, and is mediated through, 'bare' experience. If knowledge begins with experience, it can also treat experience as transparent to what lies beyond it.

It is because discerning evidence can be a matter of insight, and not just of picking up obviously observable physical chunks of stuff, that we should not regard evidence as simply moving by well-established and universally accepted rules from one bit of physical stuff to another. There is another, perhaps more important, sort of evidence. It is the evidence of things unseen or difficult to see, yet capable of transforming perceptions and lives and setting them on a journey towards infinite Goodness. For some, that will be a Platonic fall into airy nonsense. For people like me, it is the heart of wisdom, and philosophy is one way to seek it.

The final irony for those who think there is just one rational answer to every question, or who think that you have to have publicly agreed evidence for all your beliefs, is that there is no evidence to help anyone to decide conclusively whether this belief, belief in Clifford's rule, is rational or not. It follows that, if Clifford's rule ('don't believe anything without evidence') is true, then it would be wrong to accept it (because there is no evidence for it). In that sense, Clifford's rule is self-refuting. On the other hand, if the rule is not true, then there is no reason to accept it. It is very important to take all available evidence into account; but it is false to think that every meaningful question must only be answered by appeal to publicly available and irrefutable evidence.

THE ROLE OF REASON

Dialectical reason

Clifford's view is 'evidentialist', because it holds that the only acceptable form of reasoning is publicly available evidence that puts matters beyond reasonable doubt. That is an idea that many contemporaries seem to accept, but there is really nothing to be said for it. Evidentialist reason has its own proper sphere, which is the sphere of scientifically ascertainable facts. But there are many other areas of human life and experience – all the areas I have discussed in this book, in fact - where an insistence on using evidential reasoning alone would be out of place. In such areas a wider idea of reason, which I will call dialectical reason, applies. This involves the rational assessment of values and practical judgments over the whole range of personal experience, and requires a process of sensitive and imaginative balancing of differing fundamental perspectives.

Dialectical reason is what is found in Plato's Dialogues, where an attempt is made to formulate beliefs and ideas clearly and adequately, but where they are subjected to ruthless analysis and criticism. It is found in Aristotle's commendation of practical wisdom (*phronesis*). Such reason does not resolve fundamental conflicts in a neutral and conclusive way. But it helps us to make complex practical judgments in those many areas of human life where values and perspectives seem inevitably to conflict.

There are many questions that seem, as far as our present mental capacities go, to be in principle unresolvable. The list is a long one, and will include: whether humans ever possess real freedom to do otherwise than they actually do; whether mind is reducible to matter; whether materialism or idealism is the more adequate philosophy; whether democracy or meritocracy is the best social system; whether moral values are objective or subjective; whether justice is retributive or reformative; and a host of others, including the main issue of this book, whether there is a spiritual dimension to reality or not.

If you ask what the most reasonable view is on such issues, it is not sensible to say that it is the view with the best empirical evidence. They all have the same empirical evidence, and still agreement cannot be reached between equally intelligent and informed people. Yet there is a difference between unreasonable and reasonable beliefs. I suppose that reasonableness is more a matter of the way in which we form and hold our beliefs rather than a way of conclusively deciding which beliefs are true. In other words, reasoning is a procedure rather than a definite test for truth.

There are a few simple rules of reasonableness. First, a reasonable view will seek to be aware of the basic principles that the view depends upon, and to see how various other beliefs are implied by those first principles. This is much more difficult than it might seem. Few of us really trace our beliefs back to first principles, and see what those principles are. We rarely have time to think what other beliefs those first principles might lead to, if we thought them through. For instance, we might believe strongly in democracy, but never have thought through just what we mean by 'democracy' – whether it is the rule of the majority, or rather the right of the people to elect representatives who will then take the decisions. And we might not have followed through the consequences of our choice – thinking what happens if the majority wants to be ruled by a dictator, for example. Even when we do our best to get clear about these things, it is very hard to be quite sure what we think. But it is reasonable to do our best, and to see that people will disagree with us without being stupid or evil. Not only that, it will be good to face up to disagreements, because that will help us to get clearer about what we think.

If the first rule is getting clear about our first principles and their implications, this at once gives us a second rule, which is to get a fair view of beliefs that disagree with ours. This also is very difficult and rather rare. In most arguments people will misunderstand the beliefs of their opponents, and state them in stereotyped or unduly negative ways. If you listen to many Christians trying to say what Muslims think, for instance, you will very often get views that are not based on close knowledge, and that educated Muslims would never accept. The best rule here is that, when you state the beliefs of other people, you should always state them in ways that those people would accept. Do not just put your words into their mouths. This is just a simple matter of being fair and accurate, but it is also a condition of being reasonable, because it is always unreasonable to express someone else's beliefs in ways to which they would object. If they object, you cannot have stated their view reasonably. An important point to bear in mind is that other people's beliefs are usually much more complex and qualified that you give them credit for. So easy knock-down arguments against them usually miss the mark. That is a sign of unreasonableness.

Of course you cannot agree with every belief. Even when you have stated some beliefs in a way that their adherents could recognise and accept, you will often find yourself disagreeing with those beliefs. You will have criticisms of them. A third rule of reasonableness is that, if you are going to criticise others, you must allow them to criticise you with the same freedom. You must open up your own beliefs to criticism. This is also difficult, and people very often try to stop others from criticising their beliefs, even though they feel free to criticise others. That is unfair and unreasonable. The second rule will stop you mocking or simply laughing at their beliefs. But you can still bring the strongest criticisms you can to bear, on condition that you allow them to do the same to you. In fact it is a good rational principle to state outright the strongest criticisms of your own beliefs that you can think of. This is not often done in public life, and it might even be regarded as a weakness. People do not always want to be reasonable.

But if you do want to be reasonable, it is important to admit where your own beliefs seem to be quite weak. For instance, anyone who thinks the cosmos exists in order to generate valuable states must admit that the existence of immense suffering is a major weakness of their position. The only compensation is that every set of beliefs will probably have weak points, and you may be able to argue that the strengths of your position outweigh the weaknesses. But it is a sign of rationality, given the state of human intelligence, to admit you are not omniscient, that there are unresolvable disagreements between human beliefs, and that therefore you might be wrong. More than that, there will usually be some strong points in the beliefs of others, and it might be as well to try to learn from them if you can.

This, however, raises a difficulty. All of us will feel that some beliefs are morally objectionable, and need to be totally opposed. The intentional killing of innocent humans, for instance, cannot be justified for any reason – yet some people will have reasons for it (for example, they might say that the victims are genetically unfit). All you can learn from their view is how immoral humans can be. This is where reason must connect with morality. A person could carry out an immoral purpose (like exterminating an alien race) very rationally – that is, using well-devised means to that end. But you must also ask if having an immoral purpose is reasonable. It seems clear that it is always unreasonable to aim at evil for its own sake. Given a free choice, a rational person will always aim at what seems to be good to them. A rational person will also have to admit that what seems good to them must also seem good to anyone relevantly like them. If I do not want to be killed, I must, if I am reasonable, admit that no one like me wants to be killed. So if doing things to me that I do not want is bad, I must admit that, other things being equal, it is bad to do things to other people that they do not want.

Other things are not equal, of course. I may not care much about all this. Nevertheless, if I was completely rational, I would not make an exception just in my own case, and I would see that causing harm to sentient beings is bad. There is, in other words, a link between reason and morality. Anyone who was fully rational, and not swayed by desires and passions, would see that causing harm is bad and to be avoided. This gives a fourth rule of reason, that reasonable actions will aim at good, and will not cause avoidable harm. So reasonable beliefs will promote good actions or help to bring about good states, and they will avoid promoting acts that cause harm. If you have a religious or political belief that causes harm, for instance that incites people to hate or misunderstand others, that belief is irrational. Thus beliefs can and should be reasonably opposed if they promote hatred against others. But it would be self-contradictory to oppose them in ways that actually arouse hatred against those who hold them. This may seem like a counsel of perfection, since most people would think that sometimes we have to prevent harm by the use of violence. Even if that is true, we need to think very carefully about whether the use of violence is necessary, proportionate, and likely to be effective. And we need to think carefully about the sort of harm that is in question. There are no easy answers, and again there is room for differences of opinion. But it remains true that one test of a reasonable belief is the extent to which it is likely to promote good and universal human well-being, not harm and human suffering.

When we think about moral questions, there are very clear differences between the moral views of different cultures, and moral views have changed considerably throughout history. Recognition of this fact suggests that we need to be aware of the historical origin and the cultural development of our beliefs about values, and seek to see them in a fully global context. We will not pretend to have a 'view from nowhere', without any prejudice or partiality. So a fifth rule of reason is to be aware of the historical and cultural context of our value beliefs. My beliefs, for example, will inevitably be influenced by the fact that they are stated in English by an elderly white male of a certain class, and it would be unreasonable to think that this has no affect on them. What I can do about that is to try to extend my knowledge as much as possible, and be sensitive to the ways in which my historical context inevitably influences my beliefs. I cannot just give up my beliefs because of this, but I can at least be aware that they are formed within a specific perspective, that will need to be expanded and developed as time goes by. In other words, my beliefs will not be final and definitive. They may be firmly held, but they must be seen as to some extent provisional.

It is not the case, then, that beliefs are only reasonable if they are based on overwhelmingly good empirical evidence (that is evidentialism). I have suggested five major rules of reason which can and should be used in most non-scientific areas of human life and experience. First, we should aim to clarify our most basic beliefs, ensure that they are consistent in themselves and with all other well-established knowledge, and work out their main implications. Ideally, all our beliefs should be **consistent**. Second, we should try to get as fair and sympathetic an account of the beliefs of others as we can. Our beliefs should be **empathetic**. Third, we should welcome free and informed criticism of all beliefs, including our own. Our beliefs should be **critical**. Fourth, we should try to ensure that our beliefs promote human well-being and avoid needless harm. Our beliefs should be **morally fruitful**. And fifth, we should be aware of the historical context of our beliefs, aim at as wide-ranging and comprehensive a range of understanding as possible, and recognise that our own beliefs will be provisional in many respects. Our beliefs should be **comprehensive** and sensitive to their historical origins and context, with the limitations and possibilities this implies .

Formulating a reasonable view will always be a delicate matter of balance and judgment, for achieving which there is no mechanical formula. It follows that there will not usually be just one reasonable view on a contested topic. Reason, while being an invaluable rule of procedure, will not decide ultimate questions of how you interpret human existence at the most basic level. Matters of fundamental perspective lie deeper in the human heart and mind than that. Humans are axiologically oriented animals. That is, their commitments to values usually precede purely theoretical considerations. The most fundamental choices that confront all humans are whether to choose beauty, truth, creativity, empathy, and justice, or not. Those commitments precede the activities of reasoning by which people try to justify and articulate their fundamental beliefs. Humans are free agents who define their personhood by choosing ways of life and commitments to value. They are not just value-neutral calculating machines.

It is partly for this reason that there may be a number of reasonable views between which pure reason itself cannot compel a decision. It will be sensible to see your own view as a defensible one, and indeed as the most comprehensive and adequate one of which you are aware. But it will often not be sensible to see your view as one that should be overwhelmingly obvious to any intelligent person.

In this situation, the psychologist William James, in an essay 'The Will to Believe', made some suggestions about rational believing that I think still apply today. He said (though he did not use this precise term) that there are many beliefs that are essentially contested – even with all the empirical evidence to hand, there seems to be no way of establishing one interpretation that will be acceptable to all informed and intelligent people. Some of these beliefs will be 'vital' – they will be of great practical importance. Belief in the freedom of the will would be one such belief. Some will be 'forced' – we will have to decide an interpretation one way or another. We have to act either as if the will is free and people are responsible, or the will is not free and people should be treated, not punished. Some will be 'living' – they are real options for which many people believe there is much evidence, even if it does not convince everyone.[29]

I have argued that the belief that there is a spiritual dimension to reality is such a belief. There seems to be no way of settling whether this is the case or not; it makes a great difference to your life if you believe it; we either have to believe it and pray and seek to know that dimension, or not believe it and not bother to pray; and millions of people claim that their lives have been transformed for the better as a result of believing it. Perhaps that is the decisive test.

If such a belief is supportive of personal values and commitment to living a good human life, that is a good reason for accepting it, for trying it and seeing if it 'works' – if it makes for a good, happy and fulfilled life.

To commit oneself to the belief that there are objective moral goals and purposes for human life, that the cosmos in which we exist is in some way oriented to the flourishing of personal values, and that we are responsible for helping to realise them, is fully reasonable. In cases like this, moral and pragmatic reason trumps strictly evidentialist reason. Humans are feeling and willing agents in a complex and often ambiguous world. They are not disembodied calculators. Calculation, the careful weighing of evidence, is an important part of rationality. But it would be irrational to ignore the inclinations of the heart towards the good, which help to make us fully personal beings.

Common sense and spiritual sense

It is often argued that we should ignore controversial topics and just stick to common sense. But it turns out that common sense will not even support the conclusions of modern science, especially when you get to quantum mechanics and quantum cosmology. It is not really enough for philosophical reflection, either, which has to take seriously the thought that there is more to experience than appears to the unreflective eye, that reality may be more than appearance. And it is certainly not enough for serious consideration of claims about the existence of Spirit, which can affect the sort of life humans try to lead.

Is the unreflective acceptance of common sense anything more than that – a failure to reflect? All humans have to face the question of how they are going to live, and of what sort of meaning they are going to find in their lives. Humans want to know what it means to live well, how to escape from the confusions, destructive passions, and compulsions that so often beset them. So they have to reflect on what a fulfilled human life is, or whether there is such a thing. They have to ask whether there is a moral goal in life, or whether that is something you just have to make up for yourself. They have to ask whether there is a spiritual basis to reality, which might suffuse the whole of experience with a deeper and more enduring meaning.

I am not suggesting that the answer to such questions is obvious. I am suggesting that the questions are real and vital ones. If you are going to ask them, you have to be prepared to set aside preconceived prejudices and opinions – which is what 'common sense' largely is. You might, like David Hume, in the end decide that you must come back to common sense and tried and tested habits that seem to work. But you might find, as David Hume surely did, that your reflections on these topics may have life-changing consequences.

Common sense is not enough. I believe there is such a thing as true human well-being. I think it consists in overcoming the common sense view that you should take your pleasure where you can, only believing what can be tested and agreed by everybody. It consists precisely in going beyond the ordinary, in finding a deeper meaning, an objective and commanding ideal of human welfare, a purpose of finding truth, deepening understanding, appreciating beauty, aiming at unlimited compassion, and finding a happiness that does not fade or fail. It consists, in short, in liberation from the everyday.

Such things cannot be, or at any rate will not in the foreseeable future be, agreed by everybody. Such things cannot be checked by any sort of experiment, because they are only discernible by personal insight, and only checkable by personal experience, the quality of which is not testable by any quantitative experiment. In short, such things require dialectical reasoning.

Thus it is that those who say there is no evidence for God, for a mind-like basis of all beings, are restricting the word 'evidence' in a wholly unacceptable way. If you mean by 'evidence', all those experiential factors which lead to and confirm the personal discernment of Ultimate Mind, then there is abundant evidence.

And for millions of ordinary people, for most philosophers in human history, and for virtually all religious thinkers, the evidence is overwhelming.

This is the goal of the spiritual life – to know Spirit in all things, and to know all things in the Spirit. These are the forms Spirit takes in our world, and these are the evidences that Spirit is not only real, but the one enduring reality that is expressed in everything that exists, and yet is infinitely beyond anything that can ever be fully expressed and understood by us. It is, as the *Vedas* say, one reality, though it has many different names and descriptions. For some it remains un-named, even un-nameable. Some call it *Brahman*, and some the *Tao*. It is the heart of the idea of God. It remains for many millions that which is most fully real, the goal of life's greatest journey, and, so millions hope, it is what lies at last to be revealed beyond the veil of this world's time.

BIBLIOGRAPHICAL NOTES

[1]   Anselm, 'Monologion', ch. 1, and 'Proslogion', chps. 2 and 3, give a short and elegant outline of Anselm's thinking.

[2]   Locke, Berkeley, and Hume all agreed that human knowledge is constructed from 'ideas' or sense-impressions. Berkeley argued, I think successfully, that all sense-impressions are mind-constructed. Of course he accepted that there was an external world, but argued that it too was constructed and held in being by the mind of God. His widely misunderstood argument is in *A Treatise concerning the Principles of Human Knowledge*, (1710). Neither Hume nor Locke held this view in the form in which Berkeley did. So Berkeley's is not the only form of either Empiricism or Idealism by any means. But it demonstrates how easily Empiricism passes over into Idealism.

[3]   A. J. Ayer, *Language, Truth and Logic* (Gollancz, 1936). This radical distinction between objective facts and subjective values is characteristic of the Logical Positivists of the early Twentieth century – who are now virtually extinct.

[4]   The speech of Diotima in Plato, *Symposium*, trans. Walter Hamilton, (Penguin, 1973; 211a, p. 93), outlines in a beautiful way how the love of the Good and Beautiful is the highest form of human activity.

[5]   Iris Murdoch, in *The Sovereignty of Good* (Routledge, 1970), has an extended argument in favour of the objectivity of aesthetic and moral values. She does not think, however, that 'the Good' has any independent causal efficacy in the world; it is rather an object of contemplation both in art and morals.

[6]   I have tried to do this at greater length in *Morality, Autonomy, and God* (Oneworld, 2013)

[7]   G. E. Moore, *Principia Ethica* (5th edition, CUP, 1951), introduces the idea of 'non-natural facts', by which he means facts not amenable to scientific analysis, and not locatable in space-time. Mathematical and moral facts would be non-natural states that make mathematical and moral propositions true.

[8]   Immanuel Kant, in the *Critique of Pure Reason* (1781) argued that all theoretical (by which he meant scientific) knowledge needed both sensory experiences and concepts (categories) contributed by the mind. Thus the mind plays an active and constructive part in knowledge.

[9]   I show how most major philosophers in the Western tradition have argued for the existence of God (in some interpretation) in Keith Ward, *The God Conclusion* (Darton, Longman and Todd, 2009; In the USA, *God and the Philosophers*, Fortress Press)

[10]   Stephen Hawking and L. Mlodinow, *The Grand Design* (Bantam, 2010). I discuss this book, which is admittedly highly speculative, later in the text.

[11]   Arthur Peacocke, *Paths from Science Towards God*,(Oneworld, 2001). In a number of works, Dr. Peacocke uses the idea of 'top-down' or whole-part' causation, originally drawn from biology, to explain how the structure of an organic whole can affect the behaviour of its parts.

[12]   Thomas Nagel, in *Mind and Cosmos* (OUP, 2012), though an atheist, argues strongly for some form of teleology or purposiveness in the cosmos.

[13]   Paul Davies, *The Mind of God*, (Simon and Schuster, 1992), provocatively argues that the God of the physicists is superior to the God of religion. I argue, in *Pascal's Fire* (Oneworld, 2006) that they are the same thing, but seen from very different points of view.

[14]   On fine-tuning arguments, see Martin Rees, *Just Six Numbers* (Weidenfeld and Nicolson, 1999). Lord Rees, an agnostic, argues that if any of six fundamental constants of the universe were even slightly different, intelligent life could not exist. This, he suggests, is an amazing fact that science cannot fully explain.

[15]   Francis Collins, *The Language of God* (Simon and Schuster, 2007), argues that the structures of RNA and DNA, which form codes for the construction of proteins, are just too complex and organised to have arisen by chance, and they strongly suggest purpose in cosmic evolution.

[16]   Aristotle, *Metaphysics*, 11, provides Aristotle's idea of God as a perfect and self-existent being, an idea which has been enormously influential on theologians , especially in Christianity and Islam. His God does not create the universe, but the universe is somehow 'moved' by its love or desire for the perfection of God.

[17]   Ramanuja, one of the major religious writers and saints of India, held that one key text from the *Upanishads*, the revealed Scriptures of India, 'All is

Brahman', means that the whole material universe is the manifestation of self-expression of the mind of the Supreme Lord, and in that sense it is his body.

[18] Fred Hoyle, quoted in Hawking, *The Grand Design*, p. 202.

[19] W. B. Gallie wrote an influential paper, 'Essentially Contested Concepts', delivered to the Aristotelian Society, 12 March, 1956. There has been much discussion of this paper, but I just want to take from it the thought that there are a number of topics on which there seems to be no way of obtaining agreement, even among equally informed and intelligent disputants.

[20] Excellent books on the history and diversity of religions are: Ninian Smart, *The World's Religions* (CUP, 1989) and John Hick, *An Interpretation of Religion* (Macmillan, 1989). Professor Hick argues for his own 'pluralist hypothesis', that many religions are authentic paths of liberation or salvation.

[21] Brihadaranyaka Upanishad

[22] Martin Heidegger (in *Being and Time*) wrote of the 'anxiety' of human existence before the threat of non-being, and Jean-Paul Sartre (in *Being and Nothingness*) described man as a 'useless passion', holding that there is no objective purpose, value, or meaning in existence. A small but profound book, *The Courage to Be*, by theologian Paul Tillich (Nisbet, 1952), examines these analyses of human existence, and argues that they arise by failing to recognise a transcendent spiritual dimension to human life.

[23] Soren Kierkegaard, *Concluding Unscientific Postscript*, Section 2, Chapter 2, p. 203 (trans. Howard and Edna Hong, Princeton University Press, 1992)

[24] A useful and informative survey of types of spiritual experience is: Marianne Rankin, *An Introduction to Religious and Spiritual Experience* (Continuum, 2008). There is also, of course, the classic *Varieties of Religious Experience* by William James (Gifford Lectures, 1901-2; Penguin Classics, 1982)

[25] David Hume, *An Inquiry Concerning Human Understanding* [1748], Liberal Arts Press, New York, 1955, p. 123, note 1.

[26] The most infamous case is the Michael Persinger helmet. Persinger placed a helmet on the heads of experimental subjects and passed mild magnetic fields through them. He claimed to stimulate 'mystical experience and altered states'. His results have not been duplicated, and have been subjected to much criticism by neuro-scientists. Even as weak and highly disputed evidence, they would only show that some apparently perceptual mental states can be artificially stimulated, not that there are no genuine perceptions.

27   Plato, *The Republic* (Book 7, 514; trans. Desmond Lee, Penguin Classics, 1955,p. 316)

28   W. K. Clifford, 'The Ethics of Belief', in the *Contemporary Review*, 1877

29   William James, 'The Will to Believe' [1896], in *Essays in Philosophy*, ed. Frederick Burkhardt, Fredson Bowers and Ignas Skrupskelis (Harvard University Press, 1978).

Also by Keith Ward

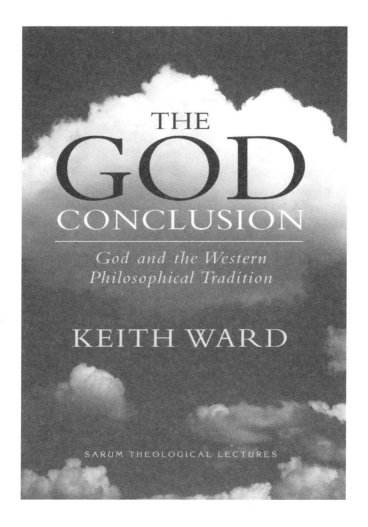

THE
GOD
CONCLUSION

*God and the Western
Philosophical Tradition*

KEITH WARD

SARUM THEOLOGICAL LECTURES

THE GOD CONCLUSION
God and the Western Philosophical Tradition

Introduction

This book defends one main thesis. It is that the Western classical tradition in philosophy – found in the works of the 'great philosophers' who would normally be studied in Colleges – accepts the God conclusion. There is a supreme spiritual (non-physical) reality which is the cause or underlying nature of the physical cosmos, and which is of great, and maybe the greatest possible, value or perfection.

The book is a defence of this thesis, because the thesis has in recent years been denied, dismissed, or simply overlooked by many writers. It is important to remember our intellectual history, and to remember that belief in God has usually been expounded by the best-known philosophers as the most rational view of the world. Such belief has hardly ever been regarded as a matter of 'blind faith' or of some irrational leap in the dark. It lies at the very basis of acceptance of the intelligibility of the universe, of the importance of morality, and of a deep understanding of the nature of human existence.

In defending this thesis, I have also taken the opportunity to defend many 'lost causes', to try to correct some widely held but mistaken ideas about what philosophers have believed, and to defend a few currently unfashionable ideas. So I hope my defence will be entertainingly provocative as well as being correct.

Thus I defend Plato against Sir Karl Popper's attack on him as an enemy of the 'open society'. I defend Aquinas' 'Five Ways' of demonstrating the existence of God. I show that Descartes was not what is usually described as a 'Cartesian dualist'. I defend (to a great extent) Bishop Berkeley's immaterialism. I attack with some vigour David Hume's arguments against God. I show that Kant did not destroy all possible arguments for God. I try to show that Hegel is not unintelligible, that Schopenhauer was not really an atheist, and that Nietzsche got into an irretrievable mess about freedom. I conclude by arguing that modern materialism is probably already out of date, and that at the very least it is an incomplete theory on a number of counts. If accepted it would of course rule out the existence of God. But I argue that it is not a strong enough theory to bring the main Western theistic tradition to an end.

The book is not really about the philosophy of religion. It is about philosophy insofar as its major concerns impinge upon religion. The connections are quite close, since some major philosophical questions are concerned with the ultimate nature of reality, the nature of the human person, questions of meaning, value and purpose, and questions of responsibility, freedom and morality.

Philosophers have something of a reputation for independence of mind and scepticism, and they usually dislike being thought of as defenders of any sort of orthodoxy. There are some notable defenders of orthodox belief, like Thomas Aquinas. But even he was banned from teaching for a while by the Bishop of Paris, and his views were thought to be very advanced in the thirteenth century.

Nevertheless it is the case that most major philosophers have inclined to a roughly Idealist view of the world – they have thought that there is something mind-like at the basis of things, or that values are in some sense objective. There has always been an anti-Idealist opposition, and it still exists today. Some of the best-known philosophers of recent times have inclined to reductionist or materialist views of one sort or another, though they are in fact a minority among professional philosophers.

I intend to treat matters historically, moving from the ancient Greeks, by way of late medieval Christendom and the Enlightenment, to recent emphasis on problems of consciousness and artificial intelligence. It may seem an unduly European or 'Western' history. But it is in Europe that philosophy, understood as the pursuit of critical and independent thinking, has flourished. It may only be part of a rich and much more varied global heritage of thought. But the problems it has dealt with, and the way in which it has dealt with them, remain characteristic of a specific tradition of thought that was born in Greece and flourished conspicuously in Europe after the Enlightenment. So it may be seen as one important tradition of human thought.

Some might hold that the tradition has now come to an end. But I think that, on the contrary, it still has a great deal of importance to contribute to human understanding of the world. I think it is vital to consider the questions about God it raises in a serious, critical and informed way, and not to let discussions about God degenerate, as these days they often do, into a conflict of unsubstantiated prejudices. I also think that philosophy, while it is serious, should also be fun. I hope it is.

The God Conclusion *is available from www.dltbooks.com or contact Norwich Books and Music on 01603 785925 or at orders@norwichbooksandmusic.com*